CREATIVE
CHRISTMAS
CRAFTS

CREATIVE CHRISTMAS CRAFTS

consultant editor

ALISON WORMLEIGHTON

photographed by

PAUL FORRESTER

RUNNING PRESS

PHILADELPHIA, PENNSYLVANIA

A QUARTO BOOK

Copyright © 1993 Quarto Inc

All rights reserved under the Pan American and International Copyright Conventions. First published in the United States of America in 1993 by Running Press Book Publishers.

9 8 7 6 5 4 3 2 1

Digit on the right indicates the number of this printing

ISBN 1–56138–294–9

Library of Congress Cataloging-in-Publication Number 93–83531

This book was designed and produced by
Quarto Inc
The Old Brewery
6 Blundell Street
London N7 9BH

Senior Art Editor Penny Cobb
Designer Nick Clark
Photographer Paul Forrester
Stylists Moira Clinch, Penny Cobb
Senior Editor Sally MacEachern
Artists David Kemp, Ed Stuart
Art Director Moira Clinch
Publishing Director Janet Slingsby

Typeset in Manchester by Bookworm Typesetting
Manufactured by Eray Scan Pte Ltd, Singapore
Printed by Star Standard Industries (Pte) Ltd, Singapore

This book may be ordered by mail from the publisher. Please include $2.50 for postage and handling. *But try your bookstore first!*

Running Press Book Publishers
125 South Twenty-second Street
Philadelphia, Pennsylvania 19103

CONTENTS

$\mathcal{D}$ECK THE HALLS

$\mathcal{T}$HE FESTIVE TABLE

$\mathcal{S}$EASONAL NEEDLEWORK

$\mathcal{C}$HRISTMAS KEEPSAKES

CHRISTMAS IS ALWAYS A MAGICAL TIME, BUT YOU CAN MAKE IT EVEN BETTER – MORE EXCITING AND MORE OF A SHARED FAMILY EXPERIENCE – BY CREATING YOUR OWN CHRISTMAS "ACCESSORIES." IT IS NATURAL TO COOK SPECIAL MEALS FOR CHRISTMAS, AND TO SPEND TIME SHOPPING FOR CARDS AND PRESENTS AND DECORATING YOUR HOME – SO WHY NOT GO ONE STEP FARTHER AND RETURN TO THE IDEA OF THE TRADITIONAL CHRISTMAS IN WHICH ALMOST EVERYTHING, FROM CARDS, PAPER CHAINS, AND TABLE DECORATIONS TO THE CHILDREN'S CHRISTMAS STOCKINGS, IS MADE BY HAND?

THIS BOOK CONTAINS A WEALTH OF INSPIRING IDEAS FOR LOVELY THINGS YOU CAN MAKE FOR THE

INTRODUCTION

FESTIVE SEASON. MANY OF THE PROJECTS HAVE BEEN INSPIRED BY THE INVENTIVE AND CRAFT-LOVING VICTORIANS, WHO MADE CHRISTMAS INTO SUCH A GREAT FAMILY OCCASION, BUT OTHERS ARE MORE MODERN IN FLAVOR, AS WELL AS IN THE TECHNIQUES AND MATERIALS USED. ALL CAN BE MADE EASILY EVEN IF YOU HAVE NO PREVIOUS EXPERIENCE OF A PARTICULAR CRAFT, AS ANY SPECIAL TECHNIQUES INVOLVED ARE QUICKLY LEARNED.

SOME OF THE PROJECTS ARE ACCOMPANIED BY FULL LISTS OF MATERIALS AND DETAILED BUT EASY-TO-FOLLOW DIRECTIONS, WHILE OTHERS ARE INSPIRATIONAL IDEAS TO GUIDE YOU ON YOUR WAY TO MAKING YOUR OWN CREATIONS. THE EMPHASIS THROUGHOUT IS ON CREATIVITY AND ENJOYMENT, SO THAT EVEN WHEN SPECIFIC MATERIALS AND COLORS ARE MENTIONED, YOU SHOULD ALWAYS FEEL FREE TO SUBSTITUTE YOUR OWN, OR CHANGE THE DESIGNS TO SUIT YOUR OWN PERSONAL TASTE.

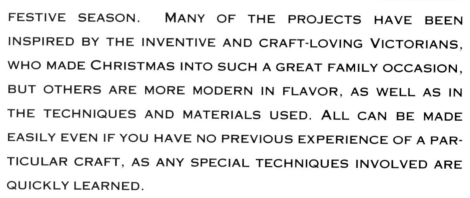

Similarly, although some of the projects specify a certain type of paint, you can often substitute one for another. All the paints used are described in the glossary, so you can turn to this first if you are not sure whether you have a suitable paint for the job in hand. The glossary also explains any sewing terms that might be unfamiliar, so you need never fear that you will be unable to complete a project.

The materials listed do not include items such as scissors and glue, which you will be using throughout the book – these are shown both here and in the introductions to each chapter. Unless a particular glue is mentioned you should use a non-toxic household glue.

REMEMBER!

And do remember the following safety tips:

• Be careful with scissors and craft knives, and do not let children use them.

• Any spray painting, varnishing, or gluing (particularly using spray adhesive) should be done in a well-ventilated room.

• Keep lit candles away from curtains, streamers, foliage, tinsel, pets, and children.

• Don't hang stockings, garlands, tinsel, cards, etc, from the mantelpiece if you plan to have an open fire.

• Holly berries are poisonous, so are best avoided if there are young children and pets in the house.

GENERAL WORKBOX
masking tape • cellophane tape • double-sided tape • felt-tip pens • pen • pencil • tracing paper • scissors • craft knife • ruler • paintbrushes • non-toxic household glue • spray adhesive

Finally, have fun making the projects. Take your time over them – remember that there will always be another Christmas – experiment and enjoy yourself.

CHAPTER ONE

Cards and Gift wraps

IN SPITE OF THE EVER-INCREASING RANGE OF COLORFUL AND WELL-DESIGNED CARDS AND WRAPPING PAPERS, THERE IS STILL NOTHING TO BEAT HOMEMADE. A CHRISTMAS CARD IS APPRECIATED SO MUCH MORE WHEN IT HAS BEEN MADE BY HAND, AND IMAGINATIVE GIFT WRAPS MAKE ANY GIFT MORE SPECIAL.

ALTHOUGH THE CUSTOM OF EXCHANGING PRINTED CARDS AT CHRISTMAS BEGAN IN THE 1840S AND WAS WIDE-SPREAD BY THE 1870S AND 1880S, HANDMADE CARDS GO BACK MUCH FURTHER. FROM THE 18TH CENTURY ONWARD, JUST BEFORE CHRISTMAS, SCHOOLCHILDREN USED TO PREPARE EXAMPLES OF THEIR BEST PENMANSHIP ON HIGH-QUALITY PAPER, OFTEN DECORATED WITH COLORED BORDERS. THESE "CHRISTMAS PIECES" WERE PROUDLY PRESENTED TO PARENTS AND GRANDPARENTS.

CARDS AND GIFT WRAPS

Gold Filigree wrapping paper (see page 20).

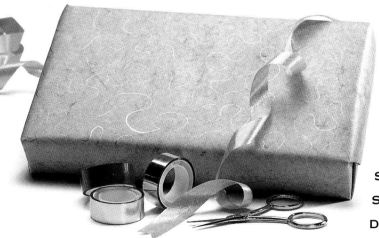

LIKE THE PRINTED CARDS, THE EXCHANGE OF GIFTS GOES BACK TO THE MID-19TH CENTURY. AT THAT TIME, WRAPPING PAPER WAS GENERALLY BROWN, SO THE GIFT-GIVER WOULD EMBELLISH IT BY HAND, WITH CUT-OUT SPANGLES, FRILLS, AND COLORFUL SCRAPS ARRANGED IN ATTRACTIVE LITTLE DESIGNS. TODAY, CARDS AND GIFT WRAPS THAT ARE HANDMADE PROVIDE THE OPPORTUNITY TO GIVE THESE TRADITIONS GREATER MEANING.

Personalize your presents with homemade gift tags cut from wrapping paper.

A fabric bow is ideal for displaying cards. Make up three double-layered fabric rectangles, bind the edges with ribbon, then sew together by hand.

$\mathcal{I}$N THIS CHAPTER YOU'LL FIND DOZENS OF PROJECTS AND IDEAS FOR ADDING YOUR OWN DISTINCTIVE STYLE TO CARDS AND GIFT WRAPS. THEY RANGE FROM QUICK, INGENIOUS IDEAS THAT CAN BE USED FOR ALL YOUR CARDS AND PRESENTS, TO MORE ELABORATE PROJECTS FOR THE SPECIAL PEOPLE ON YOUR LIST. CHILDREN CAN HELP WITH MANY OF THE PROJECTS AND WILL THOROUGHLY ENJOY SPONGING, SPATTERING, OR POTATO-PRINTING THEIR WAY THROUGH YOUR CHRISTMAS-CARD LIST. THERE ARE ALSO SOME REALLY ATTRACTIVE WAYS OF DISPLAYING THE CARDS YOU RECEIVE.

GENERAL WORKBOX
see page 7
SEWING WORKBOX
see page 77

Transform a plain box by covering it with wrapping paper. Cut out pieces for the sides, top of lid, and sides of lid, adding extra to tuck underneath or inside. Snip into these margins, apply glue to the box, and smooth the paper over it.

$\mathcal{T}$HE SELECTION OF PAPERS AND RIBBONS AVAILABLE TODAY IS AWESOME, AND THIS CHAPTER WILL SHOW YOU SOME WAYS OF USING THEM IN ALL THEIR GLORY. YOU'LL ALSO FIND LOTS OF BRILLIANT IDEAS FOR TURNING ORDINARY, EVERY-DAY MATERIALS INTO STUNNING GIFT WRAPS, BUT PERHAPS MOST IMPORTANT OF ALL, YOU'LL DISCOVER HOW TO MAKE THE PREPARATIONS FOR CHRISTMAS A TREAT FOR YOUR WHOLE FAMILY.

MATERIALS

FOR ALL CARDS
Thin cardboard in different colors

STENCILED WINDOW
Oiled manila cardboard • poster paints

CHRISTMAS TREE
Fern • silver or gold spray paint • metallic paper • ribbon or braid

POTATO PRINTS
Gouache or poster paints

PRACTICALLY A PRESENT
Wrapping paper • ribbon

3-D SCENES
Colored and metallic papers

PADDED SHAPES
Batting • fabric • braid

STAINED-GLASS WINDOW
Tissue paper

SPECIAL GREETINGS

Homemade Christmas CARDS GIVE A SPECIAL FLAVOR TO YOUR SEASONAL GREETINGS. A DELIGHT TO RECEIVE, THEY ARE ALSO FUN TO MAKE. POTATO PRINTS AND STENCILING ARE IDEAL FOR MASS-PRODUCING CARDS, WHILE OTHER IDEAS ARE MORE SUITED TO THOSE SPECIAL PEOPLE ON YOUR LIST.

STENCILED WINDOW

PATTERN PAGE 130

1 *Use the pattern and a craft knife to cut from oiled manila cardboard a stencil of a window with holly and berries.*

2 *With masking tape, mask off any areas on the stencil that are not to be a particular color. Stencil that color using thick poster paints and a stencil brush.*

3 *Remove the masking tape from the stencil and reposition to mask off other colored areas. When the previous color is dry, replace the stencil and stencil on another color.*

CHRISTMAS TREE

1 *Buy or find a fern and spray a thin layer of spray adhesive on the underside. Position on a piece of thin cardboard and press gently to ensure it is all in contact with the surface.*

2 *Spray silver or gold paint over the fern, directing the spray toward the central stem to give a "glow" around the tree.*

3 *Remove the fern, glue on a base cut from metallic paper, and edge the card with ribbon or braid.*

POTATO PRINTS

1 *Cut out 8 × 4in rectangles from bright-colored cardboard and fold the rectangles in half.*

2 *Cut a potato in half and press it against a paper towel to get rid of some of the moisture.*

3 *Cut out a simple shape (a star, Christmas tree, bell, holly) from cardboard. Using a pencil or felt-tip pen, draw around the shape onto the potato.*

4 *With a small kitchen knife, carefully cut around the shape without damaging the surface.*

5 *Dilute gouache or poster paint in a saucer and dip the surface of the potato into it. Press the potato firmly down on some spare paper.*

6 *If the shape is not fully printed, dry it off and carefully slice off the tip to give a flatter surface.*

7 *Use the potato as in step 5 to print your cards. To make the design more interesting, dip a strip of potato in paint and use it to print a border.*

STAND-UP PRESENT

1 *Cut four rectangles, each 4 × 4¾in from thin, bright-colored cardboard. Cut a diagonal slice off the tops of two of these rectangles.*

2 *Make slits as marked on the Angel pattern (p. 131), so the two complete rectangles can be slotted together and the other two pieces slotted into those.*

3 *Cut two bow shapes from thin gold cardboard, and cut one in half. Glue to each side of the top slit of the sliced rectangle. Glue the complete bow to the other sliced rectangle.*

SPECIAL GREETINGS

STAND-UP ANGEL
PATTERN PAGE 131

1 Use the patterns to cut out two large and two small triangles from thin white cardboard.

2 Cut slits where marked. The exact length of the slits will vary with the thickness of the cardboard; cut too small rather than too large, as you can always cut more later.

3 Cut off the tops of the two larger triangles.

4 Use the wing pattern to cut two wing shapes from thin gold cardboard. Glue the wings to the edge of the small triangles, about ¼in in.

5 Use the head pattern to cut two head shapes from pink cardboard. Cut one in half lengthwise and glue on top of the large triangle, on each side of the top slit.

6 Glue the complete head on top of the other large triangle.

7 Slide the two large triangles together along the slits near the edges.

8 Slide the triangles with wings together, along the slits near the edges. Attach them to the larger triangles along the middle slits.

9 To flatten the card for sending, press the two outer pieces together. To open, gently pull the outer edges apart.

STAND-UP TREE

1 Cut triangles with slits as for the Angel, steps 1-2.

2 Cut two stars from gold cardboard. As in steps 5-6 of the Angel, cut one star in half and glue to each side of the top slit on one large triangle. Glue the complete star to the top of the other.

PRACTICALLY A PRESENT

1 Glue wrapping paper to a folded card. Cut slits in it that are slightly wider than the ribbon you will be using.

2 Thread two lengths of ribbon through the slits, securing the ends firmly inside the card with glue. Finish off with a bow.

3-D SCENES

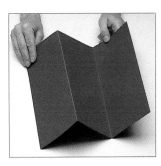

1 Cut a 12 × 8in rectangle from thin cardboard. Make two folds in the cardboard, one inward and one outward, to divide it into three equal panels, each 4in wide.

2 Lay the card flat again and cut away a triangle, beginning 4¾in down the right-hand edge and ending at the top left-hand side of the center panel. Refold the card.

3 Decorate by gluing on colored and metallic papers.

PADDED SHAPES

PATTERN PAGE 130

1 Trace a simple shape (stocking, bell, wreath) on the front of a folded card. Cut it out with a craft knife.

2 Cut a piece of batting slightly smaller than the shape and stick it on a piece of thin cardboard the same color as the main card.

3 Glue a piece of fabric onto the batting and glue to the inside of the card beneath the cut-out shape. Finish off with a braid edging, and a bow if the shape is a wreath.

STAINED-GLASS WINDOW

1 Draw or trace an angel and window panes on black or very dark cardboard.

2 Carefully cut out the window parts using a craft knife.

3 Either leave it plain or glue colored tissue paper inside to create a stained-glass effect.

ON DISPLAY

When those hordes of Christmas cards start arriving, be prepared! Make some of these attractive card holders ahead of time, so you can display all the cards to best advantage. A pair of holders look good on a mantelpiece, a shelf, or on the wall.

TRIMMING THE TREE

MATERIALS

Thick cardboard or foam board 25 × 20in • Christmas fabric: 46 × 30in • ³/₈in- wide ribbon: 3½yd • ¼in-wide elastic: 2¼yd • glittery decoration (ball or star) • self-adhesive hanger

PATTERN PAGE 133

1 *Use the pattern to cut out a tree shape from thick cardboard or foam board. Cut out the tree shape from fabric, adding 1in all around. Glue the fabric centrally to one side of the cardboard.*

2 *Clip into the corners and glue the excess fabric onto the wrong side.*

3 *Place the ribbon centrally over the elastic, allowing for 12in of ribbon to every 8in of elastic.*

4 *Pull the elastic to fit the ribbon and stitch them together down the center to gather up the ribbon.*

5 *Cut the gathered ribbon into lengths to fit across the tree at intervals as marked on the pattern. Position on the right side and pin the ends into the cardboard edges to hold.*

6 *Glue the ends to the wrong side of the tree. Sew each length of gathered ribbon to the fabric at 5in intervals across the tree.*

7 *Use the pattern to cut out another piece of fabric, adding ½in all around. Place it centrally over the back of the tree, and turn under the raw edges just inside the outer edges; glue.*

8 *Glue a glittery star or ball to the top of the tree. Stick the self-adhesive hanger to the back.*

ON DISPLAY

HOLLY LEAF

MATERIALS

Thick cardboard or foam board 25 × 18in • self-adhesive or ordinary felt 50 × 20in • ⅛ in-wide braid in two colors: 3yd of each • 2 brass curtain rings

PATTERN PAGE 133

1 *Use the pattern to cut out a holly shape from thick cardboard or foam board. Draw around this on the wrong side of the felt; cut out, adding 1½in all around.*

2 *Peel off the backing if you are using self-adhesive felt. If you are using regular felt, spread the cardboard with glue. Position the felt so it is centered over the cardboard.*

3 *Stick the raw edges to the wrong side of the cardboard. Clip the curves and corners for a smooth fit.*

4 *Pin lengths of one color of braid over the felt-covered cardboard, spacing the lines equally so that they are about 5in apart and parallel.*

5 *Add more lengths of the same color of braid at right angles, weaving them under and over the first rows. Pin into the edges of the cardboard.*

6 *Weave lengths of the other color of braid alongside the first color, weaving under the braid that the adjacent one went over and vice versa. Pin the ends into the edges of the cardboard.*

7 *Turn the holly over and stick all the braid ends onto the wrong side so they are taut on the right side. Trim as necessary.*

8 *Use the pattern to cut out another holly shape from felt. Stick to the wrong side of the board, covering the raw edges and ribbon ends.*

9 *Use the ring pattern to cut two ring sections from felt. Peel off the backing if you are using self-adhesive felt. Fit the strips through the curtain rings and stick to the back.*

10 *Glue the circles to the back of the holly for hanging.*

ALL TIED UP

MATERIALS

Standard-size sheet of wrapping paper, approximately 27½ × 19½in • thin cardboard 25 × 12in • thick cardboard 25 × 12in • synthetic raffia • plastic ring 5in in diameter • ¾yd paper ribbon

PATTERN PAGE 132

1 *Use the pattern to cut out the tie shape from thin cardboard. Glue to the wrong side of the wrapping paper. Cut out, adding ¾in on the side and base edges, and 2in at the top.*

ℱABRIC WREATH

MATERIALS

Thick cardboard 30 × 20in ● green Christmas fabric 36 × 10in ● red Christmas fabric 36 × 30in ● batting 12 × 12in ● self-adhesive hanger ● Christmas decoration

2 Cut an inverted-V shape through the paper and cardboard at each marked position.

3 Use the pattern to cut out the tie shape from thick cardboard. Place on the wrong side of the thin cardboard.

4 Fold the edges of the paper over and glue them to the wrong side of the thick cardboard, leaving the top edges free and mitering the base corners.

5 Wind the synthetic raffia around the plastic ring, fastening the ends firmly. Take the excess paper through the ring at the top of the holder and glue to the wrong side of the holder.

6 Cut a piece of wrapping paper slightly smaller than the pattern to cover the back. Glue in place, covering the raw edges.

7 Untwist the paper ribbon and tie it into a bow. Glue the bow to the top of the holder. Trim the ribbon ends and tuck inside the bow loops.

1 Using a pencil on a length of string, cut out a circle 10in in diameter and another 14in in diameter from thick cardboard.

2 From the center of each cut a 4in circle; discard.

3 Using the larger ring as a pattern, cut one ring from the red fabric, adding an extra 1in all around.

4 Glue the fabric to one side of the ring. Glue the raw edges to the wrong side. Cut out the center so the raw fabric edges match the edge of the cardboard.

5 To make the ruffle, cut out 5in- wide strips of green fabric. Cut enough strips so that when the ends are joined, the ruffle will be twice as long as the distance around the smaller ring.

6 With right sides facing, stitch the strips together end to end to form a ring. Fold it in half lengthwise, wrong sides facing. Stitch gathering threads along the raw edges.

7 Using the smaller ring as a pattern, cut out a circle of red fabric, adding ¾in all around the outer edge. Cut out the center, leaving ¾in of fabric beyond the cardboard edge.

8 Pull up the threads to gather the ruffle evenly. With right sides facing, pin the ruffle around the outer edge of the small fabric ring, so the raw edges are even. Stitch, taking a ½in seam allowance.

9 Again using the smaller ring as a pattern, cut out one piece of batting and one of red fabric to the same size. Glue the batting over the cardboard.

10 Place the fabric circle with the ruffle over the batting; pin. Glue the raw edges to the wrong side around the outer edge.

11 Glue the remaining fabric ring over the back of the cardboard ring, covering the raw edges of the ruffle.

12 Add a 1in band of glue around the center circle on the back ring. Position the smaller front ring centrally over the back ring.

13 Take the raw fabric edges of the smaller front ring through the center hole and glue to the wrong side of the cardboard. Clip into the fabric so the edges lie flat.

14 Cut another large ring from red fabric and glue it over the back to cover the raw edges. Stick a hanger to the back. Sew a Christmas decoration centrally.

HAND-PRINTED WRAPPING PAPERS

MATERIALS

*Selection of: papers •
paints • bronzing
powders • sponge • rag
• leaves • petals • gold
foil • star stickers • gold
felt-tip pen*

SWEET AND SOUR

Sugar • malt vinegar

FOILED AGAIN

*Decorate plain paper
with thin strips of gold
foil cake trim. Choose a
fairly heavy plain paper
so that the gold strips
will stay flat. Glue the
strips on, then press the
decorated paper under
heavy books or other
weights for several
hours.*

STAR STRUCK

*Stick star stickers all
over plain paper for an
instant seasonal look.*

SWEET AND SOUR

*The old-fashioned
technique of combing a
pattern in a sugar-and-
vinegar paste painted
onto paper provides
wonderful effects. You
will need large sheets of
paper that is not too
absorbent.*

1 *Make a paste of two
parts sugar to one part
white malt vinegar,
shaking it vigorously in a
jar until dissolved.*

2 *Add some water-
based paint (gouache,
poster paint, powder
paints, or watercolors) to
color it.*

3 *Using the widest
brush you have, paint the
paste all over a sheet of
paper. Leave for ten
minutes so it dries a little.*

4 *Draw a pattern in
the paste using a match,
pastry wheel, or comb
cut from cardboard.
Alternatively, block a
pattern off with a cork
or block by stamping it
on, then smudging as
you pull it away.*

5 *If you find that the
pattern does not hold
properly, leave it to dry a
little longer and try
again.*

6 *When the pattern is
complete, leave to dry
completely – this could
take about three days.*

ADDING SPARKLE

*Use bronzing powder for
a sparkly gold or bronze
effect. First paint plain
paper with a fairly
opaque paint such as
poster color, then scatter
the bronzing powder
onto the wet paint.
Experiment with
different amounts and
methods of application
such as shaking it,
sprinkling it, or rubbing
it through a sieve.*

GOLD FILIGREE

*Create a gold filigree
design on a pale-colored
parchment or elephant-
hide type of paper by
drawing a continuous
squiggly pattern with a
gold felt-tip pen. This is
easy even if you cannot
draw, as the pen runs
very smoothly.*

EVERY ANGLE

*Cut out tiny angular
shapes from gold foil and
glue them randomly over
textured or handmade
paper. Alternatively, cut
shapes from gummed
paper strips with a foil
finish (sold for paper
chains).*

PETAL POWER

*To wrap a special present
buy sheets of bright-
colored, fabric-like
handmade paper and
glue single dried rose
petals all over it. You can
glue the petals on when
the paper is flat (in
which case press the
paper for a few hours
under heavy books or
weights) or after the
present has been wrapped.*

RAGTIME

*A dappled effect is
achieved by ragging plain
sheets of thin paper. Take
a soft rag, scrunch it up
loosely in your hand and
press the surface into a
saucer of gouache or
poster paint, making sure
the cloth does not
become too wet. Wipe
off any excess paint and
gently dab all over the
paper. When the first
layer is dry, rag over
another, darker or
contrasting color and
again let it dry. Finally
apply gold or silver paint
in the same way, using a
fresh rag.*

FOILED AGAIN   STAR STRUCK   ADDING SPARKLE   SWEET AND SOUR   EVERY ANGLE   PETAL POWER

IRONING OUT WRINKLES

SPOTS AND DOTS

REPEAT MOTIFS

RAGTIME

TAKE A LEAF

CHECK IT OUT

*I*RONING OUT WRINKLES

For a textured surface, crumple up strongly colored paper into a ball. Smooth it out and spray a fine mist of metallic paint onto it at a slight angle, so that some areas catch more paint than others.

*R*EPEAT MOTIFS

Use spray paint to stencil brightly colored tissue paper with simple star, Christmas tree, and holly motifs. Choose a random, all-over pattern or formal lines or borders, letting the spray paint fall around the edge of the stencil.

CREATIVE CRINKLES

*S*POTS AND DOTS

Again using brightly colored paper, spatter thick gouache paint to create a spotty effect. Load a paintbrush (the larger the brush, the bigger the spots) with paint and flick it at the paper from a distance of about 12in. Use several colors but let each one dry before doing the next, otherwise the spots will run into each other.

*T*AKE A LEAF

1 *Use leaves and spray paint to build up an all-over, random pattern. First spray a sheet of tissue paper patchily with gold spray paint. Leave it to dry for a few minutes.*

2 *Hold a leaf against the paper and spray a little silver paint over the top.*

3 *Repeat in a random fashion all over the paper. Use a fresh leaf*

after each sheet of paper, as the paint builds up on the leaf and can drip onto the paper.

*C*HECK IT OUT

1 *Create a checked effect by first cutting strips of cardboard 1in wide and spraying one side lightly with spray adhesive.*

2 *Position the strips at 1in intervals lengthwise over the paper, making sure they are stuck down well.*

3 *Gently sponge undiluted gouache paint over the surface. Poster or acrylic paint can be used instead, but gouache gives a more attractive, opaque effect.*

4 *Remove the cardboard strips. When the paint is dry, position the strips widthwise across the paper. Sponge over them with a different-colored gouache paint. Remove the strips and leave them to dry.*

*C*REATIVE CRINKLES

Potato-printing on tissue paper, using a fairly runny water-based paint such as gouache or poster paint, creates an attractive crinkly effect. Cut a simple shape from a potato (see page 12) and

print all over the paper, either randomly or in a pattern.

RIBBON ROSE

Make a ribbon rose using wire-edged taffeta ribbon or, for a different effect, soft satin ribbon.

[1] Roll the ribbon from the middle, starting tightly then letting it loosen as you go, until you have an open rose shape. Hold the bottom tightly or it will spring undone.

[2] When the rose is big enough, staple or sew the base together, catching all the thicknesses. Tweak the "petals" out to make it look realistic.

[3] Make a small paper leaf and attach this to the gift, then glue the rose in place over it.

PAPER BOW

This red and green polka-dot bow is made from paper ribbon. The secret of dealing with paper ribbon is to use it confidently. Here one strip of ribbon is wrapped around the length of the box and a second one around the width, then a flat bow is added separately. Don't attempt to tie a bow — make it from flat pieces glued together.

TAKE A BOW

*B*OWS IN WONDERFUL COLORS AND IMAGINATIVE DESIGNS CAN MAKE ALL THE DIFFERENCE TO GIFT WRAPS. THEY NEEDN'T BE COMPLICATED — HERE ARE SOME DRAMATIC EFFECTS THAT ARE EASY TO ACHIEVE.

CLASSIC BOW

The classic tied ribbon is the plainest yet one of the most effective of all bows. For a really good finish use a wire-edged ribbon like this taffeta one – it has a good body and stays where you put it. Always trim the ends after tying.

BOWS GALORE

Use narrow ribbon to tie lots of tiny bows, or buy them readymade from notions departments, and glue them all over a wrapped present. Use just one color or lots.

𝒢AUZY RIBBON

For a glamorous effect, tie a very wide, soft, gauzy ribbon on top of a round box covered in a richly detailed wrapping paper. Let the ends float.

𝒞URLED RIBBONS

Use curling ribbon to make a basic bow, then attach extra lengths. Curl each by pulling the back edge of a scissor blade along the length.

𝒫LEATED PAPER DECORATIONS

Instead of ribbon use pleated paper strips to decorate a wrapped box.

1 Cut long lengths of paper, gluing the lengths together if necessary.

2 Fold a strip into narrow accordion pleats, squeezing hard to make the folded edges crisp.

3 Cut small lengths and glue them to the center of the wrapped package.

𝒫APER FANS

Paper fan decorations can be used on any shape of present as long as it has a flat surface.

1 Cut strips of any paper that will hold a fold well and fold each into narrow accordion pleats. Press tightly.

2 Holding the folded strip at the base, open out the top edge to make a fan. Glue the base or use a piece of double-sided cellophane tape.

3 Attach the base of the fan to the wrapped present with a dab of glue or double-sided cellophane tape along the whole base of the fan.

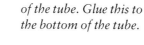

*S*EE-THROUGH
SOLUTION

Here's a pretty solution to the perennial problem of wrapping a spherical present.

1 *Place the gift on a large square of tissue paper and bring the edges to the top.*

2 *Tie tightly with string or ribbon and spread out the bunched-up paper at the top.*

3 *Cover the wrapped gift in the same way with crisp acetate or cellophane, this time tying it with a decorative cord or ribbon.*

4 *Finish with either a bright bow in a clashing color or a cord with the ends tied into knots. You could also add a tassel or*

attach beads or decorations to the ends of the cord.

*C*HRISTMAS
SPIRIT

A corrugated cardboard tube is an excellent way to wrap a bottle and can look surprisingly decorative. Use plain or colored stiff corrugated cardboard (or any thick bendable cardboard).

1 *Measure the circumference and height of the bottle, and cut the cardboard so it will be a little taller than the bottle and will wrap tightly around it, overlapping slightly.*

2 *Glue the edges of the cardboard together to make a tube.*

3 *Cut a round bottom piece of non-corrugated cardboard to fit the base*

of the tube. Glue this to the bottom of the tube.

4 *Cut a piece of corrugated cardboard which will be used for the lid. It should fit quite tightly over the main tube but be loose enough to slide on easily. Glue the edges to form a tube.*

5 *From corrugated cardboard cut a circular top to fit the lid. Glue it in place.*

*S*PECIAL
EFFECTS

*W*HY USE ONLY CONVEN-TIONAL PAPER AND RIBBON WHEN WRAP-PING GIFTS? HERE ARE SOME IDEAS FOR IMPROVISING WITH GIFT WRAPS RANGING FROM SILK AND CELLOPHANE TO BURLAP AND BEADS, PLUS SOME NOVEL WAYS OF WRAPPING DIFFICULT SHAPES LIKE SPHERES AND BOTTLES.

6 *Put the bottle inside the box, slide the lid on, and tie it securely with narrow ribbon.*

*R*OUGH WITH
THE SMOOTH

Stiff, untreated burlap, or a coarse cotton fabric provides an unusual and attractive way to wrap a bottle. Carry the natural

theme through with raffia and beads, all in earthy colors.

1 *Cut a circle of the fabric large enough to enclose the bottle and leave a small surplus at the top.*

2 *Wrap the bottle in soft tissue and stand it in the center of the circle.*

3 Draw up the edge of the fabric and gather it together, straightening out the folds of fabric around the bottle.

4 Tie the top securely with thin string or wire, then add a decorative tie of raffia. Thread beads onto some of the raffia ends.

MYSTERY OF THE PYRAMIDS

A pyramid of corrugated cardboard works well for a jar, perfume bottle, or any other small bottle. Ideally, cut the complete shape from a single piece of cardboard.

1 Stand the gift on the cardboard and mark around the base. Now draw a square enclosing the circle; this will be the base of the pyramid.

2 From the sides of the square, mark out four triangles slightly taller than the gift. These will form the sides of the pyramid.

3 Using a craft knife, cut out around the outside of the shape. Score the base with the craft knife so that the four triangles can be bent upward to meet at the top.

4 Make a hole in the tip of each triangle. Pack the present in tissue paper and put it into the pyramid. Bring the tips of the triangles together, either wiring them or tying them with thread.

5 Decorate with ribbons or wind curly decorative wire right around the pyramid from top to bottom.

BEADED TIES

Beaded ties are a novel way of tying a square or rectangular present. After wrapping the gift in any paper you wish, thread large wooden beads onto thin ribbon, string, raffia, or cord, spacing them at random. Tie each in place either by making a large knot on each side of the bead or by looping thread behind and knotting it. Do the two ties separately, crossing them over at the top and twisting them together to hold them in place.

THE SOFT OPTION

A jar of homemade preserves or a bottle can look sensational wrapped in fabric rather than paper. Use a square scarf or napkin, or cut a square of fabric. Stiff silk dupion, used here, is ideal because it has body and does not flop.

1 Cut a square of fabric large enough to cover the gift and leave a generous ruffle at the top.

2 Stand the gift in the center of the fabric square and bring all the fabric up around it, gathering it just above the top of the gift.

3 Tie tightly with string, ribbon, or cord. Make a decorative bow, if you like, with another strip of fabric.

4 You can pink the edges of the fabric, or leave them raw if they are unlikely to unravel too much. Or you can deliberately fray them for ⅛in or so to make a fringe.

SOMETHING FROM NOTHING

HERE IS A GREEN TREE THAT REALLY IS GREEN — IT'S DECORATED WITH ORNAMENTS MADE FROM RECYCLED MATERIALS, RANGING FROM PEACH PITS TO WOOD SHAVINGS.

CLOSE SHAVINGS

Now that wood shavings are used in potpourris, their decorative potential is more widely recognized. Here's a novel way of using them.

1. Buy or find coils of wood shavings, and thread conical-shaped pieces onto a length of thin wire so that they all face the same way.

2. Shape the wire into a circle and bend the ends together to form a ring.

3. Add a length of wire for hanging.

PAINTED BALLS

Spray lightweight molded balls, known as cotton balls, with metallic paint in subtle colors. If you like, add stars or another simple pattern, painted freehand. When dry, attach a hanging loop of thread or fine cord.

RECYCLED-PAPER CHAINS

Old-fashioned paper chains made from recycled paper are an attractive addition to the tree.

1. Cut recycled paper in several different colors into strips measuring ½in × 5in.

2. Form one strip into a loop, overlapping the ends and gluing them together.

3. Put the next loop through it and join the ends. Continue, mixing the colors at random or in sequence, until you have a long garland.

JUST PEACHY

Even peach and nectarine pits can be used decoratively.

1. Scrub the pits clean and leave them to dry.

2. Sponge them with gold or, if you prefer, leave them plain.

3. Glue a loop of cord to the top and decorate with a dried berry or rosehip.

UNLIKELY COMBINATION

The surprise ingredient of these delicate decorations is little tufts of pan scourer!

1. Make small bundles of twigs and glue them together.

2. Glue on a small dried apple ring (see page 66) and perhaps a small cone.

3. Add a little tuft of curly gold or copper wire cut from an old pan scourer. Tease it out to unravel it slightly.

4. Attach a thread or wire for hanging.

PICKING A SCRAP

1. Using pinking shears, cut ½in-wide bias strips of thin fabric.

2. Wrap them around a Styrofoam® ball until it is completely covered, gluing them in place.

3. Hold the last strip in place with a long pin. Use the same pin to attach a loop for hanging.

SIMPLE SEEDPODS

Tufts of pan scourer (see Unlikely Combination) can also be used to decorate other items, such as gilded seedpods. If you wish, add a little color with a rosehip or dried berry, then attach a gold cord hanging loop.

CURLY COILS

These paper coils can be thrown over the tree or looped from branch to branch.

1. Cut ¼in-wide strips of recycled paper, gluing the ends together to form long strips.

2. Roll each of these tightly around a match, securing them in place with masking tape. Leave them coiled for several hours.

3. When you are ready to use them, slide them off the stick and allow them to spring open into curly coils.

Chapter Two

Fun Decorations

DECORATING FOR CHRISTMAS IS ALWAYS ENJOY-ABLE, BUT NEVER MORE SO THAN WHEN THE CHRISTMAS DECORATIONS HAVE BEEN DEVISED AND MADE BY YOU AND YOUR FAMILY. NOT ONLY DOES THIS PROVIDE HAPPY HOURS OF OCCUPATION FOR THE PRE-CHRISTMAS EVENINGS, BUT IT ALSO ENABLES YOU TO TAI-LOR YOUR DECORATIONS TO YOUR PARTICULAR REQUIRE-MENTS, FOR EXAMPLE MATCHING THEM EXACTLY TO THE COLOR SCHEME OF YOUR ROOM.

FUN DECORATIONS

THE TREE IS, OF COURSE, THE CENTER OF ATTENTION. TRADITIONAL IN GERMANY FOR CENTURIES, IT WAS INTRODUCED TO AMERICA BY THE GERMAN SETTLERS, PARTICULARLY IN PENNSYLVANIA, ALTHOUGH CHRISTMAS TREES DIDN'T BECOME WIDESPREAD UNTIL THE 1890S. IN THOSE DAYS, AMERICAN TREES WERE GENERALLY AS TALL AS THE ROOM THEY WERE IN. THE GERMAN FASHION WAS POPULARIZED IN ENGLAND BY PRINCE ALBERT, WHO IN 1841 INSTALLED DECORATED TREES IMPORTED FROM HIS NATIVE COBURG IN WINDSOR CASTLE. THEY HAVE BEEN A CENTRAL PART OF CHRISTMAS EVER SINCE.

Beautiful Baubles (see pages 34–5).

THE TREES WERE LIT BY CANDLES UNTIL THE FIRST ELEC-TRIC "FAIRY" LIGHTS WERE INTRODUCED IN THE 1890S. (MARTIN LUTHER IS SAID TO HAVE BEEN THE FIRST TO USE CANDLES TO DECORATE A CHRISTMAS TREE, AND AN ASSOCIATE OF THOMAS EDISON IN NEW YORK CITY WAS THE FIRST TO USE ELECTRIC LIGHTS.) OTHER

VICTORIAN TREE DECORATIONS INCLUDED FRAGILE GLASS BAUBLES, OFTEN WITH FAKE JEWELS, LITTLE FABRIC SANTAS AND STUFFED TOYS, SHAPES CUT FROM TINPLATE, FOIL STARS, STREAMERS, BEADED BALLS, AND DECORATIVE PAPER CONTAINERS HOLDING CANDIES. MANY OF THESE WERE IMPORTED FROM GERMANY, BUT PEOPLE OFTEN MADE THEIR OWN.

*I*T'S JUST AS EASY TODAY TO CREATE YOUR OWN DECORATIONS – AND JUST AS REWARDING. THE PROJECTS AND IDEAS IN THIS CHAPTER REQUIRE NO SPECIALIST TOOLS OR SKILLS, APART FROM THE MOST BASIC SEWING SKILLS FOR SOME OF THE BAUBLES. THEY CAN BE MADE QUITE QUICKLY AND EASILY, MANY OF THEM BY THE WHOLE FAMILY, AND WILL ADD SEASONAL COLOR TO YOUR HOME.

*H*ERE'S THE CHANCE TO HAVE FUN USING SHIMMERING FOIL AND SPARKLY GLASS "JEWELS," FANCY BRAIDS AND FLOPPY TASSELS. FOR THE TREE, TRY THE VICTORIAN-STYLE BAUBLES AND TRULY SPECTACULAR METALLIC PAPER CHAINS. FOR A CHILD, MAKE THE SIMPLE ADVENT CALENDAR, AND FOR A HOLIDAY-SEASON PARTY MAKE SOME ATMOSPHERIC PAPER LANTERNS GLOWING WITH NIGHTLIGHTS.

On your metal (see pages 32–3).

Glowing Lanterns (see pages 40–1).

CRAFT WORKBOX
see page 93

SEWING WORKBOX
see page 77

GENERAL WORKBOX
see page 7

ON YOUR METAL

These ingenious metal-foil ornaments look terrific hanging on the Christmas tree, on a leafless branch, or in a mobile, yet they are simplicity itself to make.

MATERIALS

Metal foil (available from craft or specialist metal suppliers) in brass, copper, and aluminum • ballpoint pen • metallic thread (for hanging)

PATTERN PAGE 135

1 *Make a pattern by drawing a shape onto stiff paper and cutting it out.*

2 *Place the pattern on a piece of metal foil that is slightly larger than the pattern, and draw around it using a soft pencil.*

3 *Place the foil on a pile of magazines, with the pattern on top in the same position. Remove the ink cartridge from a ballpoint pen. Go over the outline with the pen, pressing very hard.*

4 *Remove the pattern and use the pen to draw decoration freehand onto the foil, within the outline. Remember to press hard all the time.*

5 *Cut out the design with strong scissors, and pierce a hole at the top of the decoration. Add a loop of metallic thread for hanging.*

6 *If the foil has curled, gently flatten it with a rolling pin.*

7 *The right side is the opposite side to the one worked on, which gives the metal a raised, "embossed" effect.*

JEWELED BAUBLE

MATERIALS
Styrofoam® ball • scraps of fabric • braid • beads • glass "jewels" • sequins

1 Mark the top by making a hole in the center of the ball with a small screwdriver.

2 Draw lines in felt-tip pen, beginning at the hole and dividing the ball into quarter segments lengthwise. Draw a band ¾in wide around the middle.

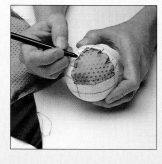

3 Using these marks as a guide, pin a piece of fabric over one of the quarter segments up to the band and draw its outline on the fabric. Cut out this shape, adding just over ⅛in all around.

4 Using this as a pattern, cut out eight segments in fabric. Cut out a band in contrasting fabric, cutting on the bias and again adding just over ⅛in to each edge.

5 Apply glue around the edges of the fabric segments and stick in place, overlapping each piece until the top and bottom of the ball are covered. Stick lengths of braid over the joins.

6 Glue a fabric band around the center. Glue a length of braid along each edge of the band. Decorate around the band with beads, jewels, and sequins.

7 Make a hanging loop out of braid and glue the ends into the hole at the top of the ball.

8 String a few beads onto a length of wire, or attach them together with thread, and sew to the center of the base.

CROWNING GLORY

MATERIALS
Colored/metallic cardboard • beads • rickrack • braid • small piece of fabric

PATTERN PAGE 134

1 Use the pattern to cut out a crown and two top pieces from cardboard. With the crown lying flat, glue on beads and rickrack.

2 When dry, form the crown into a circle, overlapping the ends. Glue the ends together, holding them with paperclips until they are dry.

3 Make a hole in the middle of each top piece, and place one on top of the other. Thread a loop of braid through the holes and tie with a knot on the wrong side to make a hanging loop.

4 Swivel the pieces to make a cross, pull through the crown from underneath, and glue the ends in the center behind each raised area.

5 Cut a circle of fabric 6in in diameter and sew running stitches all around the edge. Gather up to fit inside the crown. Glue in place.

DIAMONDS ARE FOR EVERYONE

MATERIALS
Colored/metallic cardboard • tassel • cord • braid • glass "jewels" • beads

PATTERN PAGE 135

1 Use the pattern to cut out a cardboard shape. Lightly score all folding lines. Glue the tassel inside the bottom point. Make a hanging loop from cord and glue it inside the top point.

2 Glue glass "jewels" onto the right side and leave to dry. Apply glue to the flaps and fold together to form a diamond.

3 Decorate with braid and stitch a bead to the braid at each corner.

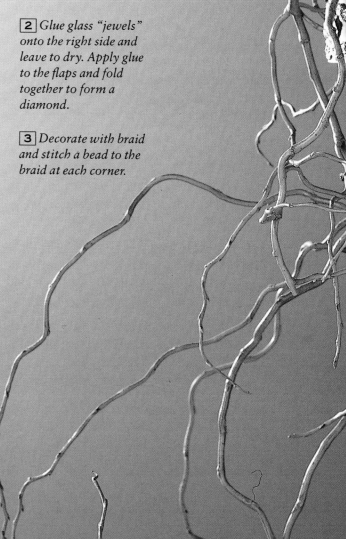

BEAUTIFUL BAUBLES

Nothing MAKES A CHRISTMAS TREE LOOK MORE SPECIAL THAN HANDMADE DECORATIONS. THE ORNAMENTS SHOWN RANGE FROM LAVENDER-SCENTED STARS TO RICHLY JEWELED BALLS. NONE IS DIFFICULT TO MAKE YET WILL ADD A TOUCH OF MAGIC TO THE TREE.

DRESSED-UP CONE

MATERIALS

Pine cone about 3in high • ½yd narrow ribbon • strip of fabric: 10¼ × 2¾in

1 Make a small hole in the center of the base of a pine cone.

2 Fold a 10in length of ribbon in half and glue the folded end into the hole in the cone. Fold an 8in length of ribbon in half and glue the raw ends into the hole to make a hanging loop.

3 Fold the fabric strip in half lengthwise with right sides facing. Stitch along the long edge taking a ⅝in seam allowance. Trim, turn right side out, and press, so the seam becomes the outer edge.

4 Turn in the raw edges at one end, then bring both ends together, pushing the raw end inside the other to make a tube. Slip-stitch in place.

5 Gather the folded edge of the tube using small running stitches and pull together to form a rosette; secure.

6 Pull the ribbons through the middle of the rosette and glue in place on the base of the pine cone. Tie the ribbon ends into a bow.

WOVEN BASKET

MATERIALS

Colored cardboard • narrow ribbon or bias-cut strips of fabric ⅜in wide

PATTERN PAGE 134

1 Use the pattern to cut out a strip of cardboard 9 × 2in. Mark the fold line and 16 lines at right angles to it. Cut each line to the fold line to make 17 flaps.

2 Fold along the fold line, snipping the folded area so it will curve around and taking care that these cuts don't join up with the flaps.

3 Cut a ⅜ × 11¼in strip of cardboard for the rim and another ½ × 6in for the handle. Use the pattern to cut two cardboard ovals for the the base.

4 Keeping the snipped, folded area flat, curve the cardboard around one base piece and glue together to form a basket. Glue the other base piece to the bottom.

5 Join the end of the ribbon or fabric strip to the wrong side of a flap with glue; leave till dry.

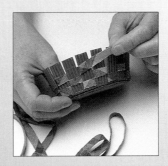

6 Weave the ribbon in and out of the flaps so the basket sides stand up, ending or gluing on new lengths as necessary. Go around the basket four times in total. Fasten off by gluing the ends at the back.

7 Curve the rim and handle pieces. Glue the rim strip around the top of the basket, and glue on the handle. Decorate with a ribbon. Fill with nuts or candy.

LAVENDER STAR

MATERIALS

Fabric: 10 × 6¾in • dried lavender • piece of ribbon

PATTERN PAGE 134

1 Use the pattern to cut out a star from thin cardboard. Draw around it on the wrong side of the fabric with a felt-tip pen to make two stars. Cut out with pinking shears.

2 Pin them together, wrong sides facing. Starting at an inside corner, hand sew or machine stitch all around, ⅛in in from the edge, ending at the last inside corner to leave one point open.

3 Stuff lightly with dried lavender then fold a piece of ribbon into a loop and pin the ends inside the open point of the star. Stitch the opening closed, securing the hanging loop.

PINK AND SILVER CHAIN

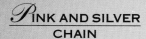

MATERIALS

Metallic paper in 2 colors

1 *Cut 2in- wide strips of metallic paper. With wrong sides facing, stick a pink strip halfway along a silver strip. Continue joining strips until you have a long length of double-sided paper.*

2 *Fold this strip into accordion pleats from one end to another; here one section (the part between one inner fold and the next inner fold) is about 5in wide. Unfold.*

3 *Using a ruler and craft knife, cut two slits in each section to within*

¾in *of the inner folds. The slits should be centered over the width of the strip.*

4 *Now carefully fold each central portion in the opposite direction to the way it was originally folded.*

5 *Refold the whole strip into pleats again and press down firmly to define the folds. Open out and twist slightly to hang, so both colors can be seen.*

PAPER CHAINS

Bring back childhood memories with these paper chains. Made from long strips of metallic paper folded in accordion pleats before being cut, they will make any room or Christmas tree sparkle.

GREEN AND SILVER CHAIN

MATERIALS

Metallic paper in 2 colors

1 Prepare and fold a strip of double-sided paper as for the pink and silver chain, steps 1-2.

2 Cut four slits over each inner and outer fold, leaving about ³/₈in between sets of slits and spacing the slits equally over the width of the strip.

3 Fold the two central portions in the opposite direction to the surrounding part, so that those cut over the inner folds are folded outward and those cut over the outer folds are folded inward.

4 Refold the strip into pleats, then unfold and hang it, as for the pink and silver chain, step 5.

STAR CHAIN AND ANGEL CHAIN

MATERIALS

Gold or silver metallic paper

PATTERN PAGE 129

1 Fold strips of gold or silver metallic paper into accordion pleats.

2 Place the star or angel pattern on the folded section and draw around it. Make sure that at least one part of the design runs right to each of the two folded edges so that the stars or angels link.

3 Using sharp scissors, carefully cut out the shape, making sure that you do not cut across the linking folds. Open out.

GLOWING LANTERNS

*M*ADE FROM TEXTURED PAPER AND LIT BY THE LITTLE CANDLES KNOWN AS NIGHTLIGHTS, THESE LANTERNS PROVIDE A MAGICAL ATMOSPHERE, ESPECIALLY WHEN USED IN GROUPS.

MATERIALS

Textured or handmade paper • silver paper • silver stars • paper ribbon to decorate • nightlights • flame-retardant spray

1 *Cut rectangles about 8 × 16in. Vary the sizes, making some taller and some wider. Some can be cut wider and then pleated.*

2 Glue a strip of paper ¾in wide to the top and another to the bottom of each rectangle to strengthen it.

3 Decorate some of the rectangles by gluing cut-out paper shapes on the inside, and decorate others by cutting out shapes from them.

4 Glue the two shorter edges of each rectangle firmly together to form a cylinder, overlapping the edges by about 1in.

5 Decorate some of the lanterns by gluing strips of silver paper to the outside in a lattice pattern, or sticking on paper ribbon and stars. Spray with flame retardant. Allow to dry.

6 Place the nightlights on a metal or foil tray, light them, and carefully place the lanterns over the top. Never leave them unattended.

MATERIALS

Thin white cardboard • shiny wrapping paper in red, green, and gold • white foam board • wrapping paper with tiny Christmas motifs (approximately 24 × 24in pieces for all the above) • 2 gold ball decorations • sequins • self-adhesive numbers • small plate hanger

GREAT EXPECTATIONS

AN ADVENT CALENDAR PROVIDES A FOCUS FOR MUCH OF A CHILD'S EXCITEMENT AND ANTICIPATION DURING THE CHRISTMAS SEASON. THIS ONE HAS A LITTLE CHRISTMAS PICTURE (CUT OUT FROM WRAPPING PAPER) INSIDE EACH OF THE **24** DOORS.

1 Cut a piece of thin cardboard 22 × 7in. Mark a grid of 1in squares on it. In the center of the second row from the top, mark a pair of 1in-wide doors.

2 In the second row from the bottom, mark three 1in-wide doors in the second, fourth, and sixth columns.

3 In the fourth row from the bottom, mark two 1in-wide doors in the second and sixth columns.

4 Repeat steps 2 and 3 in the same pattern for the remaining rows, so that you have nine rows of doors excluding the double doors at the top.

5 Glue the wrong side of the red paper to the other side of the cardboard. Cut out around the edge, allowing an extra 2in all around.

6 Cut 1in-wide strips of green paper and glue them diagonally across the red paper about 3½in apart. Working from the wrong side, cut three sides of each door.

7 Cut out and mark up one side of foam board in the same way. Cut out small motifs from wrapping paper and glue them over each marked square on the foam board.

8 Add glue to the squares not containing motifs then place the thin cardboard over the foam board so the doors align with the squares containing motifs.

9 Take the red paper to the wrong side of the foam board and glue it down, forming neat corners.

10 Cut a rectangle of red paper and glue it over the back to cover the raw edges.

11 Draw up a flame pattern and cut it out from thin cardboard. Glue gold paper onto one side; cut out, allowing an extra 2in all around. Turn these raw edges to the wrong side and glue.

12 Make a central slit in the top of the red cardboard candle. Slide the flame through it and glue in place.

13 Draw up a holly leaf pattern and cut it out twice from thin cardboard. Cover with green paper as for the flame in step 11. Stick the holly leaves to the right side of the candle base.

14 Glue the gold balls to the holly leaves. Glue a sequin to each door, then add a number centrally over each sequin. Fix the plate hanger to the back for hanging.

CHRISTMAS HEARTS

*T*RADITIONAL SCANDINA-VIAN HEARTS MAKE LOVELY CHRISTMAS DECORATIONS. THEY LOOK DIFFICULT TO MAKE BUT ARE ACTUALLY EXTREMELY QUICK AND EASY.

MATERIALS

Wrapping paper in 2 patterns or colors
• narrow ribbon
• sequins (here, leaf-shaped)

1 Cut an 8 × 5½in rectangle from each type of paper. Fold each rectangle in half lengthwise and glue together.

2 Now fold each in half widthwise and round off the two corners on the unfolded edge.

3 In each, cut four slots 3in long, starting at the fold and spacing them ½in apart.

4 Interweave the two sections. Glue a ribbon loop onto the top, covering the join with a sequin.

ALL THAT GLITTERS

FORGET SUBTLETY AND GO ALL OUT FOR A DAZZLING DISPLAY OF PURE GLITZ. THERE'S NOTHING LIKE GOLD AND SILVER FOR ADDING SPARKLE AND GLAMOUR TO A CHRISTMAS TREE.

DANGLY DECORATIONS

Use beads, pearls, and glass "jewels" as for Short and Sweet, but attach them to bows.

BEAUTIFUL BOWS

Simple bows made from glittery or metallic ribbon look stunning on a Christmas tree. Tie the ribbon in a bow, then attach a short length of florist's wire at the back of the knot and use this to secure the bow to the tree. Trim the ends of the ribbon at a slant to stop them from raveling.

SHELLS WITH A DIFFERENCE

Glue tiny artificial seed pearls and little silver or gold beads to beach-collected seashells. To hang them from the tree, attach a loop of thread, wire, or ribbon with glue.

PERFECT FOIL

Glue or wire tiny beads and fake pearls onto gold foil leaves with wire stalks (from cake-decorating suppliers). Glue a gold cord loop onto the top of each.

TINY TASSELS

Gold or silver tassels from notions departments make effective decorations used just as they are, or you can attach fake pearls, tiny beads, and bows to them. Hang the tassels on the tree by a piece of thread or wire.

SHORT AND SWEET

Make dangly decorations by threading short lengths of wire with an assortment of beads. Or tie some narrow gold ribbon around a gold-sprayed walnut and attach the beads to that. Make sure the end of the wire is knotted or wound around the last bead to hold everything in place. Tie a bold hanging loop at the top.

BEAD-DAZZLED

Thread an assortment of beads onto strong, thin wire or cord, mixing artificial pearls with metal balls, glass beads, etc. Anything light and glittery will do, so search notions departments, jewelry suppliers, hardware stores, and bead stores for items that are suitable. Hang a few short lengths of beads off the main string, and leave a wire loop at each end for hanging.

CHAPTER THREE

DECK THE HALLS

*H*OLLY, IVY, FIR, MISTLETOE, AND OTHER GREENERY ARE AN INDISPENSABLE PART OF CHRISTMAS. FROM THE SIMPLEST SPRAY TO THE MOST ELABORATE GARLAND, FROM THE WELCOMING WREATH TO THE BUNCH OF MISTLETOE, EVERGREENS PLAY A CRUCIAL ROLE IN ANY SEASONAL DECORATIONS. AND THESE ARE JUST SOME OF THE MANY WAYS OF BRINGING NATURE INDOORS AT CHRISTMAS TIME.

*B*OUGHS OF HOLLY HAVE BEEN DECKING OUR HALLS SINCE PRE-CHRISTIAN TIMES. BOTH HOLLY AND MISTLETOE WERE BELIEVED TO HAVE MAGICAL POWERS, WHILE IVY WAS ASSOCIATED WITH BACCHUS, THE ROMAN GOD OF WINE. THE CHRISTIAN CHURCH TOOK OVER HOLLY AND, EVENTUALLY, IVY AS PART OF ITS CHRISTMAS SYMBOLISM. KISSING UNDER THE MISTLETOE BEGAN IN THE 14TH CENTURY, AND THIS WAS ONE CUSTOM THAT REFUSED TO DISAPPEAR. IN THE 19TH CENTURY, EVERGREEN BOUGHS, GARLANDS, AND "WELCOME WREATHS" WERE USED ABUNDANTLY, ADORNING DOORWAYS, WINDOWS, MANTELPIECES, CHANDELIERS, MIRRORS, AND PICTURES.

*D*ECK THE HALLS

*Branching Out
(see page 65).*

*E*VERLASTING FLOWERS ALSO FORMED PART OF THE VICTORIANS' SEASONAL DECORATIONS, AND AS WE SHOW IN THIS CHAPTER, THESE CAN BE USED TO MAKE A WIDE RANGE OF ATTRACTIVE DECORATIONS. DRIED FLOWERS, LEAVES, AND SEEDHEADS ARE WIDELY AVAILABLE THESE DAYS, BUT MANY ARE EASY TO AIR-DRY YOURSELF — INCLUDING EUCALYPTUS LEAVES AND HYDRANGEA

FLOWERS, WHICH PROVIDE LOVELY, RICH BUT MUTED COLORS.

THERE IS ALSO AN INSPIRING COLLECTION OF WREATHS, GARLANDS, AND SWAGS FOR YOU TO MAKE, RANGING FROM THE TRADITIONAL TO THE UNUSUAL, AND AN EQUALLY RICH SELECTION OF SCENTED DECORATIONS SUCH AS POMANDERS. THERE ARE BRILLIANT IDEAS FOR GIVING PLANTS A SPECIAL SEASONAL LOOK, AND FOR MAKING ELEGANT DECORATIONS FROM NATURAL MATERIALS LIKE BRANCHES, TWIGS, CINNAMON STICKS, ROSEHIPS, FRUIT, AND NUTS — AND, OF COURSE, PINE CONES.

This simple spray is a charming combination of eucalyptus, gypsophila, lavender and hydrangea, but you can use dried plant material of your choice.

A basket, some teazels, and red bows make a simple, yet effective, festive arrangement.

NONE OF THE DECORATIONS IN THIS SECTION REQUIRES ANY SPECIAL EXPERTISE OR TOOLS, BUT IF YOU PLAN TO DO A NUMBER OF THE PROJECTS THAT INVOLVE GLUING HEAVY ITEMS SUCH AS NUTS AND PINE CONES, AN ELECTRIC GLUE-GUN WOULD BE A USEFUL – THOUGH NOT ESSENTIAL – INVESTMENT. GLUE-GUNS WILL FIX HEAVY OBJECTS SECURELY WITH HOT GLUE IN A MATTER OF SECONDS, THOUGH THEY ARE LESS EFFECTIVE FOR GLUING TINY ITEMS SUCH AS DRIED FLOWERS, WHERE ONLY A FINE FILM OF GLUE IS REQUIRED.

Fragrant Paper Flowers (see pages 60–1).

GENERAL WORKBOX
see page 7

FLORISTRY WORKBOX
kitchen scissors • pruning shears • bucket • toothpicks • plastic wrap • paper towels • glue-gun (optional) • florist's spool wire

WHETHER YOU DECIDE TO FILL YOUR HOME WITH FRAGRANT EVERGREENS, SPICES, AND OTHER NATURAL MATERIALS, OR JUST TO TRY ONE OR TWO OF THE IDEAS GIVEN HERE, YOU'LL FIND THIS CHAPTER AN IDEAL WAY OF CREATING THAT SPECIAL CHRISTMAS ATMOSPHERE.

EVERGREEN WREATH

Robust enough for the front door, this wreath proves that conventional does not have to mean commonplace. Its simplicity brings out the natural beauty of the foliage.

MATERIALS

Circular wire wreath frame • sphagnum moss • mossing wire • florist's wire • 3 kinds of evergreen foliage, such as blue pine, holly, and ivy (or skimmia, viburnum, choisya) • ribbon

1 *Soak the moss in a bucket of water for a few hours, then remove it and squeeze out the excess water.*

2 *Open out the moss and bind it in handfuls to the top side of the wire frame, using mossing wire and twisting the wire around the frame to begin and end.*

3 *Cut the foliage into small sprigs; pieces with woody stems should be cut on a slant to make the ends pointed.*

RINGING THE CHANGES

The traditional wreath is as much a part of Christmas as the tree. Whether as a welcoming evergreen ring on the front door or as an exquisite concoction of dried flowers hanging over the fireplace, a homemade wreath can look sensational.

4 *Bind blue pine together with florist's wire to make small bunches, leaving a long piece of wire to attach each bunch to the mossed wreath base.*

5 *Arrange each type of foliage around the base in groups to make about nine equal clumps. Position the sprigs so they overlap and all point in the same direction.*

6 *Push the woody stems into the moss and under the mossing wire. If necessary, use short lengths of florist's wire to hold them more firmly.*

7 Add all the foliage in this way. When you position the blue pine, push the wires through to the back and wind them around the wire frame, cutting off any long ends.

8 Tie the ribbon into a bow. Thread a length of wire through the back of the bow and push this through the wreath base to the back. Wind the wire around the frame, cutting off long ends.

9 Attach florist's wire to the back of the frame at the top to make a hanging loop.

*H*ERB WREATH

Here is a wonderfully fragrant alternative to the traditional fir and holly wreath.

MATERIALS
Circular wire wreath frame • sphagnum moss • mossing wire • florist's wire • fresh herbs (here, thyme, rosemary, lavender, artemisia, purple sage, bay, and myrtle) • tiny plant pots with holes in their bases • ribbon

1 Pull the wire frame into a heart shape and moss it as for the Evergreen Wreath, steps 1-2.

2 Cut any herbs with woody stems into 4in lengths, cutting the stems diagonally so that the ends will be pointed.

3 Make herbs with softer stems, such as thyme, into small bunches wound around with florist's wire.

4 Arrange the herbs in clumps around the mossed base, facing in one direction all the way around. Push the wires of the herb bunches right through to the back and wind them around the frame.

5 To wire the pots, push a length of florist's wire through the hole in the bottom. Twist the wire together on the outside, leaving a long end.

6 Dot the plant pots around the heart, attaching them in the same way as the herbs.

7 Finish by tying the ribbon into a bow and wiring it to the wreath at the top.

RINGING THE CHANGES

WREATH WITH APPLES

MATERIALS
Materials as for Evergreen Wreath • apples • pine cones • cinnamon sticks

This is a more elaborate version of the traditional evergreen wreath, featuring a classic combination of apples, cinnamon sticks, and cones.

1 Make the wreath as for the Evergreen Wreath.

2 To wire each apple, push a florist's wire through its base a quarter of the way up, then twist the wire together, leaving one long end.

3 Push another wire through the apple at right angles to the first, twisting together in the same way. Finally, twist the two long ends together.

4 To wire each pine cone, wrap a length of florist's wire around the base as close to the bottom and as far inside the cone as possible, leaving a long end sticking out.

5 Cut cinnamon sticks into 3in lengths and make into bundles held together by mossing wire wrapped around them a few times. Wrap ribbon or raffia over the wire and tie into a bow.

6 Push florist's wire through the ribbon at the back of each bundle, and twist the wire together, leaving a long end.

7 Attach the apples, cones, and cinnamon bundles to the wreath by pushing the florist's wires through the moss to the back of the wreath and twisting the wires around the frame.

NUT AND CONE WREATH

This richly textured wreath in shades of brown is a complete contrast to the more usual evergreen wreaths. It must be hung indoors, and will not be harmed by heating.

MATERIALS
Florist's-foam ring • florist's wire • selection of nuts, such as walnuts, brazil nuts, and filberts • small pine cones • ribbon

1 To prepare walnuts and brazil nuts, push a length of florist's wire into the eye of each nut and dot with glue to secure.

2 To prepare filberts, make a tiny loop at the end of a florist's wire and glue it to the nut.

3 If the cones are open enough, wrap florist's wire around each as for the Wreath with Apples, step 4. But if they are tightly closed, glue a looped end to the base of each as above. Clip all the wires to about 2in.

4 Position one kind of nut at a time on the foam base, working in diagonal bands that swirl around the ring, and packing the nuts closely together. Push the florist's wires into the foam. Continue until the wreath is covered.

5 Finish with a ribbon rosette as for the Dried-Flower Wreath, step 8.

RINGING THE CHANGES

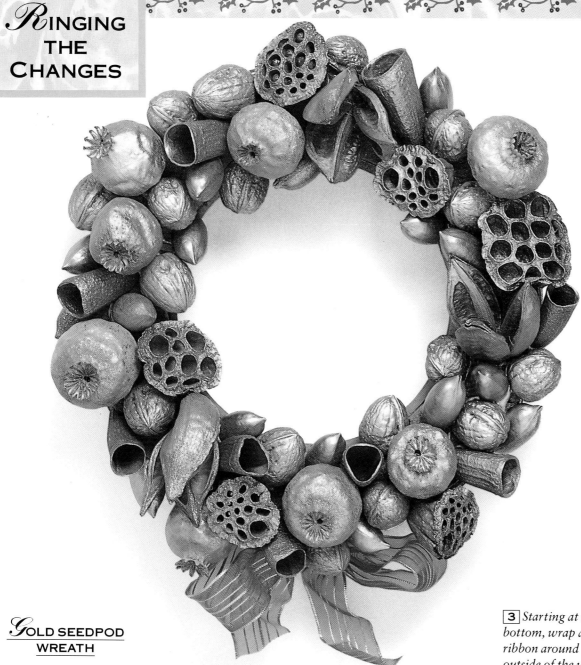

GOLD BAY-LEAF WREATH

Simplicity itself to make, this classically inspired wreath offers maximum impact for minimum effort.

MATERIALS
Twig wreath base • bay leaves • gold spray paint • ribbon

1 *Glue the bay leaves onto the twig base with the leaves all pointing in the same direction.*

2 *When the wreath is completely covered, spray it with gold paint.*

3 *Tie the ribbon into a bow and attach it as for the Evergreen Wreath, step 8.*

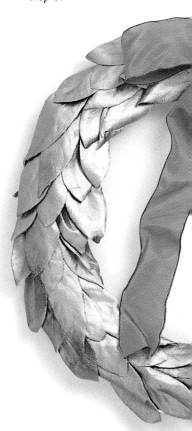

GOLD SEEDPOD WREATH

For a festive touch spray this exotic seedpod and nut wreath with gold.

MATERIALS
Florist's-foam ring • florist's wires • selection of seedpods, such as lotus and poppy • pecan nuts • gold spray paint • ribbon

1 *Push the seedpods and nuts into the foam base in a random* arrangement, *gluing in place to make them more secure. Work around the ring until it is completely covered.*

2 *Spray the wreath with gold paint, working in short bursts and building up the color.*

3 *Starting at the bottom, wrap a length of ribbon around the outside of the wreath.*

4 *Bend short lengths of florist's wire into U-shapes and push these through the ribbon into the foam around the sides.*

5 *Tie a bow where the ends of the ribbon meet at the bottom of the wreath.*

DRIED-FLOWER WREATH

Fragile flowers in delicate colors are the keynotes of this beautiful wreath. It must only be hung indoors, as it cannot withstand wind and rain.

MATERIALS

Twig wreath base (see method) • dried eucalyptus, lavender, hydrangea heads • several spriggy flowers, such as baby's breath and statice, in contrasting colors • fine wire • florist's wires if necessary • ribbon

1 When choosing a twig wreath, make sure it is loosely bound so that stems can be pushed into it easily.

2 Cut the eucalyptus into 6-8in lengths, stripping the leaves off the lower 2¾in of the stems.

3 Working around the wreath in the same direction as the twig binding, position the eucalyptus at random. Push the stems into the wreath, overlapping them as you go.

4 Divide the spriggy dried flowers into small bunches, and bind them with fine wire.

5 Dot them around the ring, pushing the stems into the wreath.

6 To hold them more securely in place you may need to twist a short length of florist's wire around each bunch, and push it through to the back of the wreath.

7 Position the hydrangea heads evenly around the wreath, pushing in the stems.

8 Make a ribbon rosette, holding it together with mossing wire. Thread florist's wire through the back, cut it to 3in and push into the wreath.

9 Make a hanging loop by threading florist's wire into the back of the wreath at the top and bending it around itself.

AMAZING GRACE

Graceful swags and garlands, sprays and bunches of mistletoe are the essence of Christmas and will give your home a traditionally festive look.

FESTOON SWAG

A swag is hung, either from two points with a curve between or in a cluster, suspended from the top. Swags hung horizontally in an elegant curve between two points are also known as festoons.

MATERIALS

Garden twine • foliage (here, box, sugar pine, eucalyptus) • spool wire • twigs • florist's wire • dried seedheads • cinnamon sticks • braid • ribbon

1 Cut a length of garden twine twice the required length of the festoon. Fold it in half.

2 Cut the foliage into pieces about 6in long. Group the thinner foliage into bunches of several stems each, wiring the stems together. The thicker foliage is used singly.

3 Twist the end of the spool wire around the double length of twine.

4 Bind the stems and bunches of foliage onto the twine, laying them so they point toward the beginning and overlap, and arranging the foliage in blocks approximately 5in deep.

5 Push pieces of twigs into the foliage. Bend florist's wire into "U" shapes and push these over the flower stems and through to the back of the swag. Twist the ends together, cut them short, and push them back into the swag.

6 Wire dried seedheads to the swag as above. Bind bundles of cinnamon sticks together with braid and attach these to the swag in the same way.

7 At each end of the swag, attach a hanging wire and a bow.

*R*USTIC SWAG

This Rustic Swag could be extended to form a garland, as the same techniques are used for both garlands and swags.

MATERIALS

Garden twine • foliage (here, fir, viburnum and rosemary) • spool wire • large poppy seedheads • long twigs • small straw wreaths • ribbon • florist's wire

1 Make the swag as for the Fir and Cone Garland, steps 1-4.

2 Use florist's wire to wire seedheads, bundles of twigs, and straw wreaths with ribbons tied around them onto the swag, as for the Festoon Swag, step 5.

3 Attach a wire for hanging at the top back. Finish with a bow as for the Fir and Cone Garland, step 6.

*F*IR AND CONE GARLAND

The terms "garland" and "swag" are often used interchangeably, but technically a garland is long and flexible enough to wind around a banister or newel post, trail around a fireplace, or even just twist into a wreath (also known as a circular garland).

MATERIALS

Garden twine • foliage (here, fir, laurustinus and rosemary) • fine reel wire • fir cones • stub wires • ribbon

1 Cut a length of garden twine twice the required length of the garland. Fold it in half.

2 Cut the foliage into pieces about 6in long. Group the thinner foliage such as rosemary into bunches of several stems each, wiring the stems together. The thicker foliage is used singly.

3 Twist the end of the reel wire around the double length of twine.

4 Bind the stems and bunches of foliage onto the twine, laying them so they point toward the beginning and overlap, and arranging the foliage in blocks approximately 6in deep.

5 Wind a florist's wire around the base of each cone (see page 53) and arrange the cones in groups of three along the garland. Push the wires through to the back, and fasten off the ends.

6 Tie the ribbon into bows and attach a wire to the back of each. Join them onto the garland as for the cones.

✿LOWER SWAG

Like the Rustic Swag this swag could be lengthened to form a garland.

MATERIALS
Garden twine • foliage (here, fir, viburnum, rosemary) • spool wire • fresh flowers (here, white tulips) • florist's wire • ribbon

1 Decide what length the swag will be, then make it as for the Fir and Cone Garland, steps 1-4.

2 Cut the stems of the flowers short and wrap the cut ends in small pieces of wet paper towels. Cover these with plastic wrap. Push the flowers in among the foliage.

3 Attach foliage with florist's wire as for the Festoon Swag, step 5.

4 Attach a wire for hanging at the top back. Finish with a bow as for the Fir and Cone Garland, step 6.

SEASONAL POTPOURRI

Try to make this potpourri six weeks before you plan to use it. This gives the fragrance time to develop. The less common ingredients are available from specialist florists and herbalists.

MATERIALS

1oz cinnamon sticks • dried peel of six oranges and four lemons • 2oz golden mushrooms • 3oz dried marigold heads • 2oz dried lemongrass • handful of dried, scented geranium leaves • ½oz star anise • ½oz powdered gum benzoin • 1 tablespoon allspice • 1 tablespoon ground ginger • 1 teaspoon concentrated orange oil • ½ teaspoon concentrated lemon oil

1. Combine cinnamon sticks, orange and lemon peel, mushrooms, marigold heads, lemongrass, geranium leaves, and star anise.

2. Mix the gum benzoin, allspice, ginger, and oils together. Sprinkle over the other ingredients.

3. Place in an airtight container (not metal or plastic). Leave in a warm, dark place.

FRAGRANT PAPER FLOWERS

MATERIALS

Paper ribbon in two widths • star anise • fine florist's wire

1. Cut two pieces of the wider paper ribbon into 9in lengths.

2. Gently untwist each length of ribbon at one end and open it out flat, forming a fan shape.

SPICE OF LIFE

A LOVELY WAY TO ADD CHRISTMAS ATMOSPHERE TO YOUR HOME IS WITH THE DELICIOUSLY SPICY SCENT OF FRAGRANT POTPOURRIS, POMANDERS, AND SPICE BALLS.

3 Glue the two together around the fan-shaped edges, leaving the bottom end open.

4 Cut a length of the narrower ribbon, and untwist it completely.

5 When the glue is dry, fill the holder with potpourri, twist the open end into a long stem, and tie the narrower ribbon around the stem.

6 Wire the star anise to the front of the holder.

Pomanders

Pomanders must be made several weeks in advance and then will last for years.

MATERIALS

Oranges or other small citrus fruits • whole cloves • ground cinnamon and allspice • ground orrisroot • narrow ribbon

1 Wrap two lengths of narrow masking tape around the fruit from top to bottom, dividing it into four segments.

2 Push cloves into the fruit, placing them close together. You may need to make holes with a needle. Avoid splitting the skin – all holes must contain a clove or the fruit could go moldy.

3 Remove the tape. Mix together a generous quantity of ground spice and orrisroot in equal parts and place in a bowl. Roll each pomander in this until it is coated.

4 Wrap each pomander in tissue paper and put in a dry, warm, dark place for three or four weeks.

5 Tie a length of ribbon around one of the channels and pin it at the top. Tie a second length around the other channel, tying it at the top and forming a hanging loop.

Spice Balls

If Christmas is upon you and you haven't had time to make pomanders, here's a quick alternative.

MATERIALS

1 Styrofoam® ball • whole spices such as cloves, peppercorns, cardamoms, juniper berries, allspice, or star anise • narrow ribbon or cord • rosehip, rosebud, or other decoration

1 Apply glue to a small area of the ball. Sprinkle or place the spices at random or in neat rows, until the whole ball is covered.

2 Glue on a hanging loop of cord or ribbon, along with a colorful decoration.

MINIATURE TREE

This is a simple yet effective idea. Use a single small tree, or line up a row on a mantelpiece, shelf, or windowsill.

Repot a small growing tree (or trees) into a terracotta pot, covering the soil with fresh moss. Attach a wide ribbon or paper bow to the pot with wire, glue, or double-sided tape. You can also add tiny bows or decorations to the tree.

POT LUCK

THE LONG-LASTING COLOR AND FRAGRANCE OF POT PLANTS MAKE THEM IDEAL CHRISTMAS DECORATIONS. HERE'S HOW TO GIVE THEM A FESTIVE, SEASONAL LOOK.

IVY STAR

This dramatic decoration never fails to look sensational. If your ivy looks a little thin, you can supplement it by twining some cut ivy around the star.

1 *Take six straight sticks of equal length, and glue them into two triangles.*

2 *When dry, lay one over the other in a star shape. Glue them together at the points where the twigs meet, then bind these joints with short lengths of natural raffia.*

3 *Bundle four to six other sticks together to make a stem, tying them*

with wire. Attach the stem to the star with glue and raffia.

4 Stick the stem of the star tree into a terracotta pot filled with soil.

5 Plant a small-leaved ivy with about five long trails and twine the ivy around the stem and through the star. Trim away any leaves around the stem of the star. If the ivy does not stay put, bind it to the twigs with thin wire in a few places.

6 Decorate the star with Christmas ornaments. Cover the soil in the pot with fresh moss.

Painted Pots

Terracotta plant pots can be made to look very festive.

1 Sponge the pots first with green acrylic paint.

2 Cut star and moon shapes out of paper to use as stencils.

3 Lay the stencils on the pots at random intervals, sponging through them with gold paint. Vary the stencil position regularly.

4 Spray varnish if you wish when the paint is dry.

Tulips in Tissue

Flowering bulbs add a lovely touch to the house at Christmas, and you can make them more special with a ruffle of bright tissue paper. (This is also a good way to gift-wrap any kind of plant in a pot.)

1 Combine two colors of tissue paper in layers.

2 Wrap the paper around the pot to fit but not quite overlap at the front, so that the plant shows. Be bold, grasping the paper firmly and squeezing it into place.

3 Secure the paper immediately with cellophane tape, then tie a satin bow around the base of the pot.

ℬRANCHING OUT

𝒞ONTRASTING WITH TRA-DITIONAL GREENERY, A NICELY SHAPED BARE BRANCH — LEFT NATURAL OR SPRAYED GOLD, SILVER, OR WHITE — IS A PERFECT FOIL FOR DELICATE ORNAMENTS SUCH AS THESE DECORATED HAND-BLOWN EGGS.

Branch

Choose a branch with a nice shape. A leafless branch has a striking simplicity, but lichen, catkins, or a few small leaves add interest.

Materials

Attractively shaped branch • gold, silver, and/or white spray paint (optional) • plant pot • quick-setting cement

[1] Either leave the branch natural, or spray it with gold or silver paint, or a combination of both. White can be used for highlights.

[2] Set the branch into the pot with cement. To keep it in position while the cement dries, support it with a web of masking tape across the top of the pot. Remove the tape when the cement is set.

[3] Add tiny gold decorations, such as star stickers stuck back to back, or decorated blown eggs.

Decorated Eggs

Materials

hen, duck, or goose eggs • paints • varnish • decorations such as glitter, braid, ribbon, gummed paper shapes, flower stamens (from cake-decorating suppliers), beads, sequins, dried or pressed flowers, cut-out pictures for découpage, velvet, lace, or other fabric scraps

[1] Keep the eggs at room temperature for at least four hours before blowing them.

[2] Pierce a hole in each end of the egg with a sharp needle or skewer. Insert the needle or skewer through a hole and break up the egg inside.

[3] Insert a straw and blow out the yolk and white, catching them in a dish.

[4] When empty, wash out the egg with disinfectant, and rinse well. Leave to drain and dry.

[5] Paint the egg. You can use any type of paint. If you use a water-based paint, it's a good idea to apply a base coat of white acrylic first.

[6] You will need several coats of paint to achieve a really lustrous finish. Allow each coat to dry before applying the next.

[7] Apply several coats of varnish, choosing the type recommended for your chosen paints, and allowing it to dry between coats.

[8] Using white craft adhesive, glue on the decorations. A découpage egg should be varnished after the pictures are glued on.

[9] Sparkly eggs look very festive. Try drawing a pattern at random in glue, then sprinkling glitter over it.

[10] Knot a length of cord for a hanging loop and glue it into the hole at the top of the egg. Cover this hole and the one at the bottom with sequins or other trimmings.

Nature's reds and greens

Dried eucalyptus leaves and apple rings threaded onto wire look very festive. They may be hung as garlands or swags or made into wreaths.

1 Pull off some large, fresh eucalyptus leaves, thread them onto a length of florist's spool wire, and hang them somewhere warm to dry for several days.

2 Use small red or green apples for the dried apple rings. Do not peel or core them. Cut them crosswise (so the core and seeds form a star in the center) to a thickness of about ¼in.

3 As you slice the apples, put them straight into a brine (saltwater) for a few minutes to stop them from discoloring.

4 Remove and thread the slices onto thick, pliable wire, spacing them out so the air can get to them. Hang in a warm place to dry for about a week. They will have a leathery texture, rather like chamois.

5 Remove the leaves and apple slices from the wires. Thread them alternately onto a length of florist's wire.

6 If you wish, you can intersperse other things such as fresh cranberries, dried flowers, or popcorn between the apples and leaves.

Natural Selection

Materials collected from gardens and hedges, orchards, woods, and fields can make wonderful Christmas decorations. A hint of gilt, a colorful ribbon, or a thin gold cord is often all that is necessary to transform them.

Moss roses

This arrangement gives a whole new meaning to the term "moss roses"!

1 Fill a plastic plant pot with dry florist's foam. Using mossing wire, cover the entire pot with sphagnum moss.

2 Push short lengths of cinnamon sticks and the stems of dried red roses and dried lavender into the top of the pot.

RUSTIC BASKET

A large rustic basket filled with pine cones, spices, and other natural ingredients makes a lovely Christmas decoration. A basket that dips down at the front and that has a handle will look best.

1 Work from the side the basket will be viewed from. Using a glue-gun, attach clusters of dried hydrangea, small roses, or other dried flowers around the inside edge.

2 Add pieces of reindeer moss at the base of the basket.

3 Begin to fill the basket with nuts, pine cones, dried seedheads, bundles of cinnamon sticks, etc. Don't pile it up too much – you should be able to see each thing clearly.

4 As a finishing touch, tie a large bow at the base of the handle at the front of the basket. Use a stiffened or wire-edged ribbon so that the bow is fat and generous.

3 Make small bows from ribbon and attach lengths of florist's wire to them. Push the wires into the foam all around the edges and among the roses.

4 Fill gaps between the roses with more moss. You can add drops of an essential oil for extra fragrance if you wish.

Natural Selection

Cinnamon Basket

This basket is the ideal decoration for cinnamon lovers. It's made from long, fat cinnamon sticks (available from florists' suppliers) and filled with spices and nuts – such as filberts, almonds, brazil nuts, walnuts, and pecans.

[1] Use a black or brown plastic flower pot as the base. Cut cinnamon sticks to length and glue-gun them all around the outside of the pot.

[2] Inside the container make a platform from floral foam or cardboard, so you won't have to fill the whole pot.

[3] Glue nuts and spices at random all over the inside of the container, building up layers so it looks quite dense.

[4] If you wish, small loops of gold ribbon or braid can be tucked in among the nuts and spices to add interest. The cinnamon sticks can be tied in bundles with gold cord.

[5] To finish off the cinnamon basket, tie a ribbon around it.

Nut and Spice Wreath

A fragrant nut and spice wreath can be hung vertically or placed flat on a table, perhaps filled with candles or fresh greenery.

[1] Glue the nuts and spices straight onto a Styrofoam® ring base (the type designed for dried flowers).

[2] Cover the Styrofoam completely except for the underside. Attach some smaller nuts and spices to other, larger nuts to build a three-dimensional effect.

[3] Either leave the nuts and spices natural or, for a glossy effect, spray them lightly with varnish.

TWIGS IN A STARRING ROLE

Twigs and ribbon complement each other beautifully in this star-shaped container. The ribbon is woven in and out of the twigs as they are attached to the container.

1 *Using a readymade star-shaped cardboard box (or other shape if you prefer), cut twigs to the same height as the sides of the box.*

2 *Glue pairs of twigs to the outside of the box, attaching the end of a length of ribbon under the first pair. The ribbon should be long enough to weave completely around the box and tie in a bow.*

3 *Continue gluing twigs in pairs, twining the ribbon over and under them alternately until you have worked right around the box.*

4 *Fill the bottom of the box with cardboard or florist's foam, then glue-gun nuts, dried chilies, and other spices all over this platform, so they are slightly higher than the edges of the box.*

5 *Spray varnish lightly over the nuts and spices.*

PLATE OF GOLD

Arrange yellow or golden fruits in a single layer on a large, shallow plate. Sponge or brush a little gold paint onto some of them to reinforce the theme. Here, Physalis and a dried magnolia leaf are added to persimmon, passion fruit, tamarillo, and pale lychees.

SUMPTUOUS WREATH

A wreath doesn't have to be green to look Christmasy. This one features dried leaves (collected in fall then pressed dry and flat), dried eucalyptus and apple rings (see page 66), little clusters of hydrangea florets and other dried flowers, and berries, nuts, and spices. All are attached with a glue-gun to a readymade twig wreath. The leaf stalks are tucked in among the twig stems of the wreath, but everything is glued securely in place.

BOLD DISPLAY

Pile a mixture of painted wooden fruits and real fruits and nuts into a shallow basket to make a bold display. Here, fresh apples, pears, tamarillos, and lychees are combined with pecans, filberts, and wooden fruits.

FRUIT AND NUT CONES

If you make two of these decorations they can stand as a pair on a mantelpiece or shelf. Pecans, filberts and almonds in their shells, lychees, and small kumquats are all suitable.

1 *To make one fruit and nut cone, trim a florist's-foam cone to fit tightly inside a small twig wreath.*

2 *Using a glue gun, attach rings of nuts and fruits, working from the bottom upward. Make the rings as neat as possible, with just one type of fruit or nut (or two alternating) per ring.*

3 *Lightly sponge a little gold paint onto some of the surfaces.*

4 *Slice off the point of the foam cone to make a flat area, then glue a whole walnut to it.*

SHAKER SIMPLICITY

A wooden Shaker-style box looks good just filled with pine cones. Wash and dry an assortment of large and small ones, and glue-gun them into place to keep them secure. Paint half a dozen of the cones with gold paint or lacquer (or buy cones already gilded) and glue them among the plain ones. You could add a ribbon or paper bow, but it also looks stylish left plain.

It's a Natural

A tree trimmed with decorations made only from natural materials provides a refreshing change from the commercial and synthetic ornaments so widely available today. Touches of gold will complement the natural colors perfectly.

MINIATURE POSIES

Make dainty and colorful decorations by tying together little posies of hydrangea florets, a pressed fall leaf, dried roses, and a few dried berries or rosehips, using fine florist's wire. (The hydrangeas also look good on their own.) Leave a short length of wire to attach the bunch to a branch, or tie on a loop of thread for hanging. They look best tied close to the fir branch rather than hanging off it.

CINNAMON ROLLS

Cut short lengths of cinnamon sticks and tie them tightly together into a bundle or a roll with wire, twine, cord, or thread. Attach a loop of wire or cord for hanging.

METALLIC LEAVES

Gauzy leaves sprayed with gold or silver make incredibly delicate ornaments (see page 127, Leaf Filigree for the method). Alternatively, you can spray-paint whole leaves and string them together.

PAINTED PINE CONES

Wash and dry pine cones, then, when they are dry, spray or paint them gold. Attach a loop of ribbon, cord, or thread to the base, using glue or thread.

CHINESE LANTERNS

Fresh or dried, Physalis makes attractive decorations. Spray the papery calyx with just a touch of gold when orange, and gild completely when dry.

GILDED LYCHEES

Gilding turns lychees into exotic ornaments. Either sponge on gold paint, or apply transparent paint medium or clear varnish then sprinkle with bronzing powder while it's still sticky. Glue a hanging loop of gold cord to the top, and add dried hydrangea florets, a rosebud, or a dried berry as a finishing touch.

TIED TEAZELS

Tie dried teazels or other seedheads together with gold ribbon, making a hanging loop with the ribbon.

DECORATIVE WALNUTS

Whole walnuts make attractive tree ornaments – simply tie gold cord around them, making a loop on each for hanging.

GOLD SEED BALLS

Glue mustard seeds or peppercorns onto lightweight balls made of Styrofoam® or cotton then spray them gold. Glue a gold hanging loop to the top of each.

CORDED LEMONS

Dry unwaxed lemons by leaving them for a couple of weeks in a warm place; piercing them with a hole near the top will hasten the process. (Dry more than you need, as some will probably just go black.) When dry, tie gold cord around them, gluing it in place and making a loop at the top for hanging. Top with a couple of tiny hydrangea florets.

CHAPTER FOUR

SEASONAL NEEDLEWORK

*I*F YOU ENJOY NEEDLEWORK, CHRISTMAS PROVIDES AN IDEAL OPPORTUNITY TO TRY OUT YOUR SKILLS IN SOME NEW WAYS, AND CREATE CHRISTMAS ACCESSORIES WITH A PERSONAL TOUCH. CHRISTMAS STOCKINGS, FOR EXAMPLE, THE HIGH-SPOT OF THE DAY FOR CHILDREN, PROVIDE ENORMOUS SCOPE. IN THE EARLY 19TH CENTURY, THESE WERE OFTEN REAL STOCKINGS WHICH CHILDREN HAD OUTGROWN AND WHICH WERE THEN DECORATED WITH EMBROIDERY AND TRIMMINGS; LATER IN THE CENTURY THEY WERE SOMETIMES MADE FROM NEEDLEPOINT. THE STYLISH STOCKINGS IN THIS CHAPTER ARE BASED ON ONE SIMPLE DESIGN, WHICH CAN BE DECORATED IN A VARIETY OF WAYS.

*S*EASONAL NEEDLEWORK

*T*HE CHRISTMAS TREE SKIRT CAN ALSO BE FINISHED IN SEVERAL DIFFERENT WAYS, INCLUDING APPLIQUÉ AND TOPSTITCHING. CHOOSE COLORS TO MATCH OR COMPLEMENT YOUR DECOR, PARTICULARLY THE CARPET, AGAINST WHICH IT WILL BE SEEN.

*I*N THE OLD DAYS, PEOPLE SOMETIMES MADE CHRISTMAS WALL BANNERS AND DECORATIVE EDGINGS FOR THE MANTELPIECE OR FOR SHELVES, AND THIS IS ANOTHER TRADI-

Mantelpiece Edging (see pages 78–9).

SEWING WORKBOX
scissors • pinking shears • needles • thread • sewing machine • glue • pins

TIONAL IDEA YOU CAN ADAPT TO YOUR OWN HOME. THE WALL BANNER AND TARTAN MANTELPIECE EDGING IN THIS CHAPTER ARE BRIGHT AND CHEERFUL MODERN VERSIONS OF THESE TRADITIONAL DECORATIONS, BUT YOU CAN CHOOSE YOUR OWN COLORS, AS WITH THE TREE SKIRT.

Counting the Days (see pages 86–7).

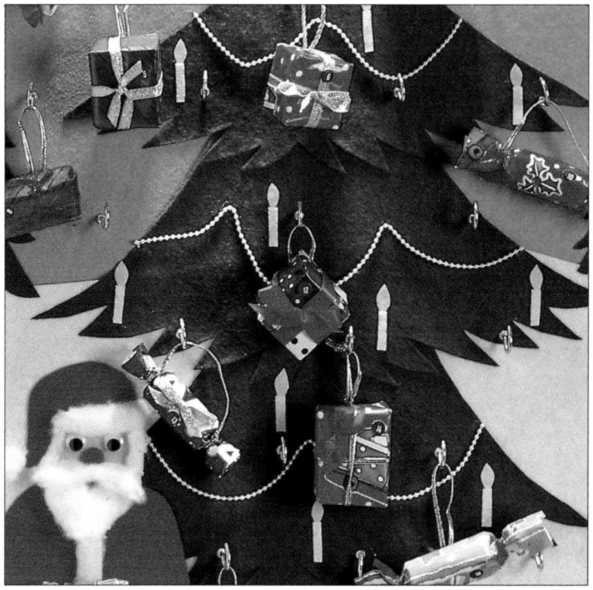

OUR BRIGHT FELT ADVENT CALENDAR IS A COLORFUL ADAPTATION OF AN OLD CHRISTMAS TRADITION, AND THIS DOESN'T NEED MUCH IN THE WAY OF SEWING SKILLS – ALL YOU NEED TO DO IS SEW SANTA'S SACK TOGETHER.

WHETHER YOU HAVE YEARS OF SEWING EXPERIENCE OR CAN SEW ON THE OCCASIONAL BUTTON, YOU WILL ENJOY MAKING THESE PROJECTS. EITHER KEEP THEM AND USE THEM YEAR AFTER YEAR, OR GIVE THEM AS GIFTS FOR FAMILY AND FRIENDS. THEY WILL ALL MAKE DELIGHTFUL PRESENTS, AND SERVE AS A REMINDER OF THE DAYS WHEN GIFTS WERE ALL THE MORE TREASURED BECAUSE THEY WERE MADE BY HAND.

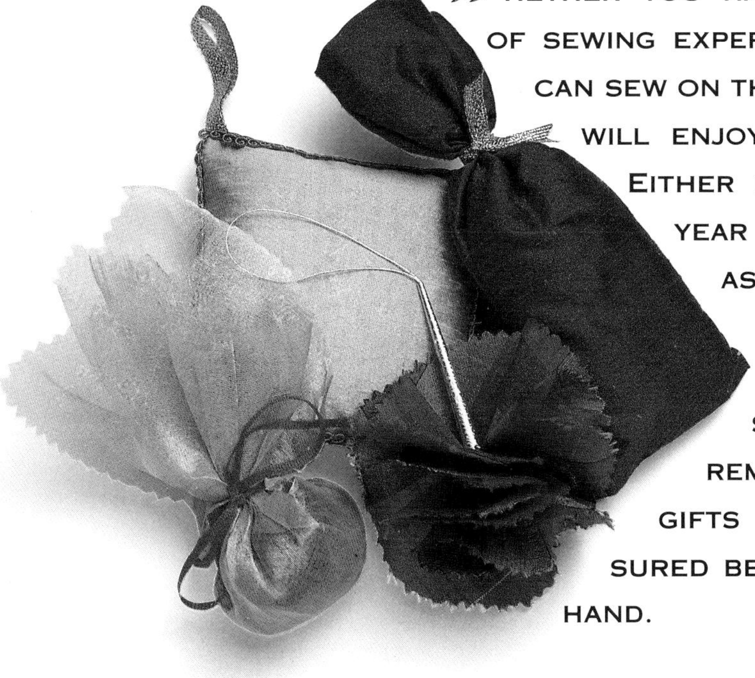

Miniature Pillows, Money Bags, Bags of Color and Pompoms (see pages 90–1).

FOCUS ON THE FIRESIDE

*T*HE FIREPLACE IS THE FOCAL POINT OF THE ROOM, PARTICULARLY AT CHRISTMASTIME, AND THIS TARTAN EDGING WILL ENSURE THE MANTELPIECE IS WORTHY OF ATTENTION. IT IS ALSO PERFECT FOR TRIMMING A DRESSER OR A SHELF.

*M*ANTELPIECE EDGING

MATERIALS

Fabric (here, tartan) • felt • fusible interfacing • ribbon in three different widths: here, 1³⁄₈in, ⁷⁄₈in, and ⁵⁄₈in • stick-and-sew touch-and-close tape

PATTERN PAGE 137

1 *Draw up a pattern for the drops. Cut out the felt drops with pinking shears. The finished length of the edging will be the length of the mantelpiece or shelf, including sides. You may want to alter the width of the drops, or the space between them, so they can be equally spaced.*

2 *Using plain scissors, cut out the tartan drops, adding ⁵⁄₈in all around for the seam allowance. Press this to the wrong side on the side and base edges.*

3 *Center the tartan drop over the felt drop with the top edges even, leaving a ¹⁄₄in felt border around the tartan on the side and base edges of the drop. Topstitch.*

4 Cut out tartan strips 2⅝in wide. Sew them together to make one strip the length of the mantelpiece plus a ⅝in seam allowance at each end. Make a facing in the same way.

5 Cut out and fuse interfacing to the wrong side of the band. With right sides together, join the band and facing along the top edge.

6 Open out the faced band and stitch the "sewing" half of the touch-and-close tape to the right side of the facing (keeping it clear of the seam allowances along the base and sides).

7 Turn under the seam allowances on the sides and base of the facing.

8 Position the drops equally along the band (leaving seam allowances at each end of the band). The top edge of each drop should be even with the raw edge of the band. Stitch in place.

9 Slip-stitch the sides and base of the facing to those of the band. Topstitch along the top and base edges of the band.

10 For every drop, one rosette is made from each width of ribbon. Cut an 18in length of the widest ribbon, a 12in length of the medium one, and a 9in length of the narrowest one.

11 Using matching thread, hand-sew running stitches along one long edge of ribbon. Pull up into a rosette shape and secure the thread, turning raw edges to the wrong side.

12 Sew three rosettes in descending size down each drop.

13 Stick the opposite half of the touch-and-close tape to the edge of the mantelpiece or shelf. Press the two halves together to hang.

SPELLING IT OUT

GUARANTEED TO RAISE A SMILE, THIS WHIMSICAL WALL BANNER WILL PUT EVERYONE IN THE RIGHT FRAME OF MIND FOR CHRISTMAS. HANG IT ON THE WALL OR ACROSS A DOOR — IT WILL IMMEDIATELY CATCH EVERY EYE.

MATERIALS

Plain fabric in two colors: each 40 × 18in ●
polyester stuffing ●
1³⁄₈in-wide ribbon ●
2 small picture-hanging rings

PATTERN PAGE 136

1 *Use the patterns to cut out two pieces of fabric for each letter, adding ⅝in all around for seam allowances. Use one color for "N" and "E" and the other color for "O" and "L."*

2 *For the letters "N," "E," and "L" place the fabric pieces with right sides together. Stitch all around, leaving an opening where shown in each for turning right side out and stuffing.*

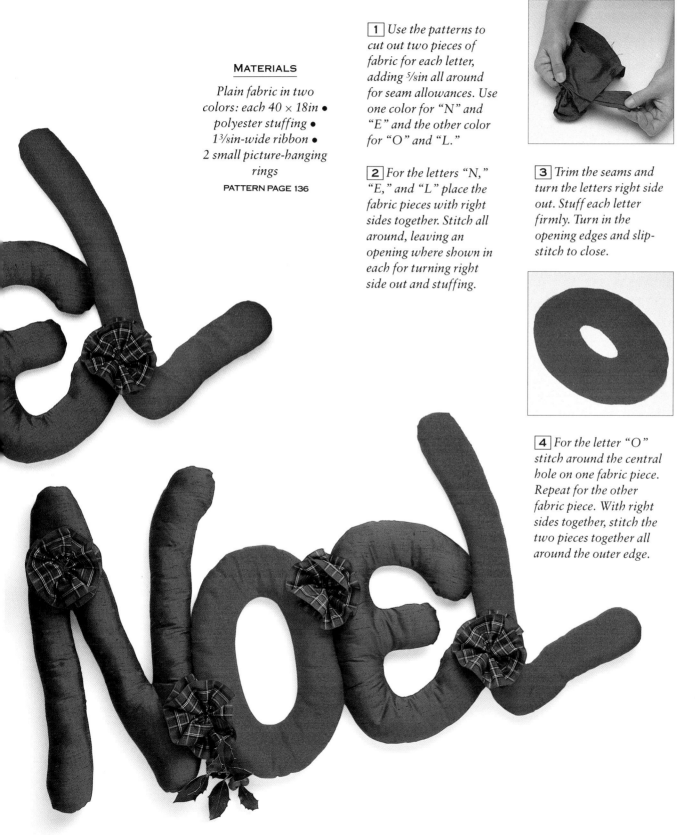

3 *Trim the seams and turn the letters right side out. Stuff each letter firmly. Turn in the opening edges and slip-stitch to close.*

4 *For the letter "O" stitch around the central hole on one fabric piece. Repeat for the other fabric piece. With right sides together, stitch the two pieces together all around the outer edge.*

5 *Trim the seam, turn the letter right side out, and stuff. Turn in the inner edges along the stitching lines around the central hole, pin, and slip-stitch.*

6 *Slip-stitch the letters together to spell "NOEL."*

7 *Make up four rosettes from the ribbon as for the Mantelpiece Edging, steps 10-11. Sew one to each letter. Sew a small ring to the back at the top left and another at the top right for hanging.*

STUNNING STOCKINGS

Make one of these cheerful stockings for every member of your family and you won't want to take them down! Bedecked with bows, stars, checks, stripes, beads, or braid, the stockings make lovely decorations in themselves.

Stunning Stockings

MATERIALS

FOR EACH STOCKING
Main fabric: 27½ ×
21½in piece • lining
fabric: 27½ × 21½in
piece • appropriate trim
(see method) • batting
(see Quick Quilting)

PATTERN PAGE 137

Snow-White Damask

SEE PAGES 82–3

1 Use the pattern to cut out two stocking pieces in the main fabric and two pieces in the lining fabric. Cut a rectangle of the main fabric 2½ × 8in for the hanging loop.

2 Place the main fabric pieces together, right sides facing, and stitch around the edge, taking a ⅝in seam allowance and leaving the top open.

3 Trim the seam and clip the curves of the heel, toe, and foot top. Turn right side out. Press the seam flat.

4 Stitch all around the top opening ½in from the edge. Turn to the inside along this guide line; press.

5 For the hanging loop, fold the fabric rectangle in half lengthwise, right sides together, and stitch down the long edge, taking a ⅝in seam.

6 Trim the seam allowance to ¼in. Turn right side out and press flat. Fold in half to form a loop. Pin to the top back edge of the stocking and stitch in place.

7 Make the lining as for the main fabric, steps 2-3, but don't turn right side out. Stitch a guide line as step 4, but turn the seam allowance to the outside.

8 Push the lining inside the stocking. Pin around the top opening and slip-stitch in place.

9 Sew a taffeta bow in place below the hanging loop.

Stripes and Checks

SEE PAGES 82–3

1 Cut out as for Snow-White Damask, step 1.

2 Use the pattern to cut out four cuff pieces in ticking. With right sides facing, pin two cuff pieces together and stitch down both side edges to make a tube.

3 Trim the seam allowances and turn the tube right side out. Press the seams flat. Pin, then stitch ribbon and rickrack in place 1¼in in from the lower edge.

4 Stitch the other two cuff pieces together in the same way but leave them wrong side out and undecorated.

5 With right sides facing, stitch the cuff tubes together along the decorated edge. Trim the seam and turn right side out. Press and baste the raw edges together.

6 Stitch the main stocking pieces together, trim the seam, clip the curves, and turn right side out as for Snow-White Damask, steps 2-3.

7 Pin the cuff in place along the top edge and stitch through all thicknesses ½in in from the top edge. Turn in the seam allowance and press.

8 Pin and stitch the hanging loop in place and complete the stocking as for Snow-White Damask, steps 7-8.

STAR-STUDDED TICKING

1 Cut out as for Snow-White Damask, step 1.

2 Cut out stars in red felt using the pattern. Arrange them on the main stocking pieces and stitch or glue in place.

3 Complete the stocking as for Snow-White Damask, steps 2-8.

ON EDGE

1 Make as for Stripes and Checks but do not decorate the cuff at step 3.

2 When complete, slip-stitch cord all around the stocking and cuff edges.

HOT MADRAS WITH BOWS

SEE PAGES 82–3

1 Make as for Snow-White Damask, steps 1-8.

2 Arrange ribbon bows on the stocking and sew them in place.

BRAID AND BEADS

1 Make as for Stripes and Checks, but decorate the cuff with gold rickrack sewn on in diagonal lines at step 3.

2 To complete the stocking, stitch gold beads along the edge of the cuff.

PRESENTS GALORE

1 Cut out as for Snow-White Damask, step 1.

2 Decorate one main stocking piece with ribbon parcels. For each ribbon parcel you need a 3in piece of 2¼in-wide ribbon, and two pieces of narrow ribbon 7in and 6in long.

3 To make each parcel, turn under ³⁄₈in on the two raw edges of the piece of wide ribbon, and pin in place on the stocking.

4 Pin one end of the longer piece of narrow ribbon to the center of the bottom edge of the parcel, tucking the end inside.

5 Leaving the top edge open, stitch the parcel in place along the other three edges. Place a small piece of folded fabric inside the parcel to lightly pad it.

6 Pin the top edge, tucking the shorter length of narrow ribbon in at the center. Stitch to close the top. Fasten the ribbon into a bow on each parcel.

7 Complete as for Snow-White Damask, steps 2-8.

QUICK QUILTING

SEE PAGES 82–3

1 Cut out the main pieces as for Snow-White Damask, step 1.

2 Cut out two stocking pieces in thin batting. Pin each to the wrong side of the main fabric pieces and baste together. Stitch with diagonal lines.

3 Make up the stocking as for Snow-White Damask, steps 2-8, but don't turn under the top edge of the main fabric or lining.

4 After pushing the lining into the stocking, bind the two thicknesses of fabric together along the top edge with strips of fabric cut on the bias, stitching the hanging loop into the seam.

MATERIALS

Paint • colored interfacing, or felt, in blue, white, green, yellow, red, and beige: ¹⁄₂yd • bulletin board with wooden frame, overall size 23 × 15¹⁄₂in • 1¹⁄₂yd fine bead trim • ¹⁄₂in brass hooks: 24 • sequins • cotton • pair of ³⁄₈in joggle eyes • scraps of wrapping paper • ribbon and string • tissues • self-adhesive numbers • gold braid

PATTERN PAGE 138

1 *Paint the frame if desired. Cut a 11 × 14in piece of blue interfacing for the sky; glue to the top half of the bulletin board. Cut a 12 × 14in piece of white interfacing for the snow; glue it to the bottom half.*

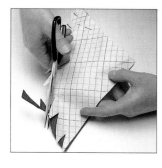

2 *Use the pattern to cut out four tree sections from green interfacing. Glue them to the left side, beginning with the base and working up the tree, with each section overlapping the next.*

COUNTING THE DAYS

*F*OR MANY CHILDREN, CHRISTMAS ISN'T COMPLETE WITHOUT AN ADVENT CALENDAR FOR THE BIG COUNTDOWN — AND THIS MUST BE THE ULTIMATE ADVENT CALENDAR WITH ITS JOLLY SANTA AND TINY WRAPPED PRESENTS FOR EACH OF THE TWENTY-FOUR DAYS. YOU CAN START WITH ALL THE PRESENTS ON THE BOARD AND UNWRAP ONE EACH DAY, OR YOU CAN PUT THEM UP ONE BY ONE AND UNWRAP ALL OF THEM ON CHRISTMAS DAY.

3 *Draw two half-trees freehand and cut them out of green interfacing. Glue these onto the background.*

4 *Cut ³⁄₄ × ¹⁄₄in strips of white interfacing for the candles and glue them to the main tree. Draw flames freehand and cut them out of yellow interfacing; now glue the flames to the candles.*

5 *Glue the bead trim across the branches. Screw in the brass hooks at random across the board.*

6 *Cut two star shapes from the white interfacing. Glue them together so the points alternate and then glue sequins around the outer edge. Glue the star to the top of the tree.*

7 *Using the Santa patterns, cut out one body and one hat in red interfacing and one face and two hands in pink. Glue the body over the face and add the hat. Glue the hands behind the sleeve ends.*

8 *Glue cotton to the head for Santa's hair and beard and to the jacket front and cuffs for fur. Glue on the eyes. Cut out a ³⁄₈in circle of red interfacing for Santa's nose; glue in place.*

9 *Glue Santa to the board 4¹⁄₄in up from the bottom edge.*

10 *For his sack cut an 11 × 4¹⁄₂in piece of beige interfacing. Fold it in half, right sides together, and stitch the side edges. Turn the sack right side out.*

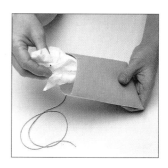

11 *Fill the sack with tissues and gather up the top, tying it with string. Glue the sack to the background and fasten Santa's arms around the top.*

12 *Wrap 24 tiny presents. Add a loop of ribbon to every present. Stick a number on each and hang from the hooks.*

13 *If desired, decorate the frame with fine gold braid.*

A SKIRT
FOR THE TREE

This is a marvelous way to cover up the pot or stand supporting the Christmas tree. If you want a larger skirt, just measure how much farther you'd like it to extend and add that to the 18in radius for the arc drawn in step 1 of the Plain Skirt.

MATERIALS

BASIC SKIRT 36IN IN DIAMETER
*45in- wide fabric: 1¼yd
• 4½yd bias tape •
hooks and eyes •
ribbons or touch-and-close fastener*

SKIRT WITH BOWS
1¼yd tartan fabric

SKIRT WITH HOLLY LEAVES
*Patterned Christmas
fabric • fusible web
• red beads*

PLAIN SKIRT

1 *Fold the fabric in half lengthwise and then in half the other way. Use a pencil on a length of string to draw an arc 18in from the folded corner that is the center point of the fabric.*

2 *Draw another arc from the same point but measuring 2in.*

3 *Cut out through all layers of fabric along both marked lines. Before opening it out, cut from the outer edge to the inner edge along one fold. This will be the center-back opening.*

4 *With right sides together, stitch bias tape to all raw edges. Press to the wrong side and hem in place by hand. Attach fastenings to the center-back opening.*

SKIRT WITH BOWS

1 *Make the skirt as for the Plain Skirt, binding the bottom edge with tartan fabric.*

2 *For each bow, cut two pieces of tartan fabric, each 12 × 4in, and cut another piece 12 × 1½in.*

3 *Fold one of the wider pieces in half lengthwise, right sides together. Stitch along the raw edges, taking a ¼in seam allowance.*

4 *Turn the tube right-side out and position the seam so it runs down the center of one side. Press.*

5 *Fold the raw edges of the tube to the center, with the seam on the inside and overlapping the ends slightly. Pleat it into three folds at the*

center and stitch securely, forming a bow.

6 *Repeat steps 3-5 for the other wide piece of fabric, then sew the two bows together at the center.*

7 *Make the remaining piece of fabric into a tube as in steps 3 and 4. Cut off a 2in piece and set it aside.*

8 *Fold under one corner of each raw end and stitch, creating a diagonal shape. Fold the length in half and, matching the centers, place it under the bows to make two tails.*

9 *Wrap the 2in length around all thicknesses at the center. Fold the raw edges under and stitch securely on the wrong side. Stitch to the tree skirt.*

SKIRT WITH HOLLY LEAVES

SEE MAIN PICTURE

1 *Make the skirt as for the Plain Skirt, using green fabric and binding the bottom edge in red.*

2 *Fuse the web onto the patterned Christmas fabric and then cut out holly leaves from it.*

3 *Arrange the leaves in clusters of four around the bottom edge of the skirt, and iron on. Stitch around the leaves using a close machine zigzag stitch to cover the raw edges.*

4 *Sew three red beads onto each cluster of leaves.*

TOPSTITCHED SKIRT

1 *Make the skirt as for the Plain Skirt, using green fabric and binding the bottom edge in red.*

2 *Topstitch the skirt in red in a grid pattern to resemble quilting lines.*

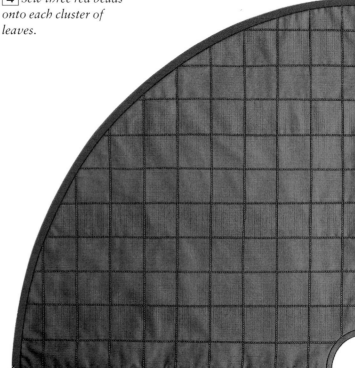

MATERIAL ADVANTAGES

*S*CRAPS OF COLORFUL FABRIC CAN BE USED IN DOZENS OF DIFFERENT WAYS TO BRIGHTEN UP A CHRISTMAS TREE. EITHER MAKE A FEW OF THE IDEAS SHOWN HERE AND COMBINE THEM WITH OTHER ORNAMENTS, OR DO ENOUGH TO DECORATE AN ENTIRE TREE.

FABRIC BOWS

Bows made from stiff fabric with a gloss or sheen, such as the metallic organdy used here, look very stylish.

1 For each bow cut a long strip of fabric, either on the bias or on the straight grain.

2 Fold it in half lengthwise, right sides facing, and stitch along the long edges. Turn it right side out. Tuck in the raw ends and stitch.

3 Tie the fabric into a bow and attach a wire to the center.

PRETEND CRACKERS

These are miniature versions of English Christmas crackers.

1 For each "cracker," make a tube of fabric, as for Fabric Bows, steps 1-2 but a little wider.

2 Tie narrow ribbon or wire around one end, a little way in from the edge.

3 Stuff the center with batting, cotton, or loose grains.

4 Tie more ribbon or wire around the second end, to keep the filling in place. Attach to the tree with thin wire.

MINIATURE PILLOWS

Square "pillows" are simple to make and, if you use striking fabrics, surprisingly effective.

1 For one pillow, cut out two squares of fabric.

2 With right sides facing, sew them together along all four sides, leaving a small opening on one side. Turn right side out.

3 Stuff the pillow with polyester filling, then sew up the opening.

4 Sew cord or braid around all four edges, and attach a ribbon loop at one corner.

MONEY BAGS

Choose a fabric like organdy that allows the colorful contents to show through.

1 For one bag, cut out a square of organdy with pinking shears.

2 Place little pieces of scrunched-up fabric, or a small piece of batting, in the center of the square.

3 Wrap the organdy around the filling, then tie a contrasting narrow ribbon around the bag, spreading out the bunched-up fabric at the top.

POMPOMS

These are made using metal cones (available from bead stores and jewelry suppliers).

1 For each pompom, cut out six to eight circles of fabric, using pinking shears.

2 Fold each of these circles into a cone shape. Sew all the pointed ends together at the bottom.

3 For the hanging loop, thread a length of gold thread through the metal cone, then secure it by sewing one end to the little holes at the wider end of the cone.

4 Sew the pompom to the cone through the same holes.

BUTTERFLY GARLANDS

Use any slightly stiff fabric, such as taffeta.

1 Cut out small rectangles of fabric using pinking shears.

2 Tie a long ribbon or cord around the center of one piece of fabric. Continue until the garland is the required length.

TARTAN TWISTS

These colorful fabric twists are quick to make.

1 Cut a strip of fabric, then use pinking shears to cut the strip into rectangles.

2 Tie gold cord around the center of each rectangle, forming a hanging loop at the same time.

BAGS OF COLOR

These simple bags look good plain, or they can be decorated with tassels, sequins, or pearls.

1 Cut out two rectangles of fabric. With right sides facing, stitch them together along one short and two long sides. Turn right side out.

2 Turn the raw edges of the unstitched side to the inside to make a neat edge. Partially stuff the bag and tie braid above filling.

CHAPTER FIVE

THE FESTIVE TABLE

FOR ADULTS, CHRISTMAS DINNER IS THE CLIMAX OF THE SEASONAL FESTIVITIES, AND IT WILL BE EVEN MORE ENJOYABLE IF THE TABLE SETTING LIVES UP TO THE OCCASION. IN THIS CHAPTER YOU WILL FIND EVERYTHING YOU NEED – BAR THE FOOD, OF COURSE – TO MAKE YOUR TABLE A VISUAL FEAST.

ALTHOUGH FEASTING HAS LONG BEEN ASSOCIATED WITH CHRISTMAS AND, BEFORE THAT, WITH MIDWINTER FESTIVALS, THE TRADITIONAL CHRISTMAS DINNER WE ENJOY TODAY DATES ONLY FROM ABOUT THE MID-19TH CENTURY. THE VICTORIANS REVIVED MANY OLD CUSTOMS BUT ALSO INVENTED MANY NEW ONES.

THE FESTIVE TABLE

TRADITIONAL BRITISH CHRISTMAS CRACKERS, FOR EXAMPLE, EVOLVED AROUND THE MIDDLE OF THE CENTURY AFTER A LONDON-BASED APPRENTICE CONFECTIONER CALLED TOM SMITH COPIED SOME BONBONS WRAPPED IN TWISTS OF TISSUE-PAPER, WHICH HE HAD SEEN IN PARIS. ONLY LATER, IN RESPONSE TO FALLING SALES, DID HE DEVELOP THE CRACKERS THAT ARE IN USE TODAY, ADDING A SMALL EXPLO-SIVE CHARGE — ALONG WITH JEWELRY, SMALL VIALS OF PERFUME, AND TINY BUNCHES OF FLOWERS.

Going with a Bang (see pages 108–9).

IF YOU MAKE YOUR OWN CRACKERS, YOU CAN FOL-LOW TOM SMITH'S EXAMPLE AND ENCLOSE ALL MANNER OF SMALL NOVELTIES. YOU'LL ALSO FIND A WEALTH OF OTHER

IDEAS IN THIS CHAPTER. FOR EXAMPLE, THERE IS ELEGANT TABLE LINEN YOU CAN MAKE BY STENCILING, A MUCH QUICKER METHOD THAN EMBROIDERY.

𝓕OR THOSE WHO LIKE TO SEW THERE ARE SOME LOVELY PLACE-MATS FEATURING SIM-PLE PATCHWORK OR APPLIQUÉ, AND FOR THOSE WHO DON'T, THERE ARE IDEAS FOR QUICK AND EASY FESTIVE PLACEMATS, DELIGHTFUL IMPROVISED NAPKIN RINGS, AND CHINA DEC-ORATED WITH CHRISTMAS MOTIFS.

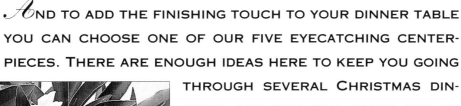

Napkins, Star-spangled Table Linen (see pages 96–7).

𝓐ND TO ADD THE FINISHING TOUCH TO YOUR DINNER TABLE YOU CAN CHOOSE ONE OF OUR FIVE EYECATCHING CENTER-PIECES. THERE ARE ENOUGH IDEAS HERE TO KEEP YOU GOING THROUGH SEVERAL CHRISTMAS DIN-NERS, AND YOU CAN ADAPT ANY OF THEM TO SUIT YOUR PERSONAL TASTE AND DECOR.

Fruit and Flowers (see page 105).

GENERAL WORKBOX
see page 7

SEWING WORKBOX
see page 77

CRAFT WORKBOX
knitting needle • plastic wrap • toothpick • plastic • screwdriver • paperclips

MATERIALS

Bought tablecloth or fabric • bought napkins or fabric • oiled manila cardboard • gold spray paint

TABLECLOTH

1 *First make the stencil by drawing a grid of lines on oiled manila cardboard. A piece about $23\frac{1}{8} \times 16\frac{3}{8}$in is ideal. You do not need to fill the cardboard.*

2 *Work out how far apart the lines will need to be, and how far from the edges, for the size of the tablecloth. Here, the lines going one way were 6in apart and those at right angles were half that.*

3 *Trace an eight-pointed star onto alternate points where the lines meet, as shown. Cut out with a craft knife.*

4 *Spray the back of the card with spray adhesive and position on the tablecloth. Mask off all around the stencil using sheets of paper and masking tape.*

STAR-SPANGLED TABLE LINEN

Sophisticated as it looks, this beautiful stenciled tablecloth with coordinating napkins is actually an ideal project for beginners. The decorated linen should be washed only by hand in lukewarm water. The metallic effect will gradually fade through several washes, but the linen should nevertheless look good for at least two Christmases. After that, it can be re-stenciled.

5 *Ensure the cloth is completely covered and check for any small gaps. Make sure the stencil is well stuck onto the cloth. If the star points are not firmly stuck down, their edges will be fuzzy.*

6 *Holding a can of gold spray paint directly above the stencil, spray in short bursts over the stars. Spray patchily so the density of the paint will vary.*

7 *Remove all paper and masking tape and carefully pull the stencil off the cloth.*

8 *Reposition the stencil, laying the outer line of stars on the stencil over the stenciled ones on the cloth to achieve the correct spacing.*

9 *Mask off the rest of the cloth again and spray. Repeat until the whole tablecloth is patterned.*

10 *When the paint is dry, if you are making your own tablecloth, hem the edges.*

11 *Press over a dry dish towel to protect the paint finish.*

NAPKINS

1 *If you are making your own napkins, cut squares of fabric about 16in wide.*

2 *Cut a piece of oiled manila cardboard about 2in smaller all around than the fabric.*

3 *Trace a row of eight-pointed stars (slightly smaller than those used on the Tablecloth) about $2\frac{1}{2}$in from the edges and that same distance apart.*

Cut them out with a craft knife.

4 *Cut a star in the bottom left-hand corner in line with the star above, and the same distance from the edge, to act as a positioning guide.*

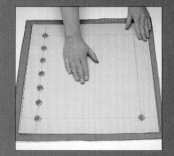

5 *Spray the back of the stencil with spray adhesive and place the stencil in the center of the napkin. Make sure there is an even margin all around the stencil.*

6 Mask off, spray with gold paint, then remove the paper and peel off the stencil, as for the Tablecloth, steps 4-7.

7 Position the stencil along the next edge, lining up the stars on the top and bottom left-hand side of the stencil with the sprayed stars.

8 Mask off again and spray once more. Repeat on the remaining edges of the square. Finish as for the Tablecloth, steps 10-11.

PATCHWORK STAR MAT

CUTTING OUT

1 On cardboard draw a square pattern and a triangular pattern, both with 2¾in sides plus a ¼in seam allowance all around. Cut out the patterns.

2 For the perimeter of the star cut out eight triangles and four squares from red fabric, and eight triangles from patterned fabric.

3 For the center of the star cut out two triangles each from the red and patterned fabrics, and four triangles from the green fabric.

4 For the border cut two pieces of patterned fabric each measuring 11 × 3in.

5 For the binding cut two strips of patterned fabric each 16 × 3in, and two more strips each 12 × 3in.

6 For the backing cut one piece of red fabric 16 × 11in.

METHOD OF WORKING

1 When piecing, all the patches are sewn with right sides together, either by machine or by hand, taking a ¼in seam allowance.

2 Take care to match any seams and always press the seams open after stitching. These steps are essential for a good finish.

PIECING THE STAR

1 First join a red triangle and a patterned triangle to form a square. Repeat to make eight squares in total.

2 Join pairs of squares to make four rectangles, with the red triangles together in each rectangle.

3 Join a red square to each short side of two rectangles. These form the top and bottom rows of the perimeter. Set aside the remaining two rectangles, which will be the sides of the perimeter.

MATERIALS

ONE PLACEMAT SIZE 16 × 11 IN

IN ANY OF THESE DESIGNS

Red fabric 45in wide:
⅓yd ● patterned fabric
45in wide: ⅓yd ● scraps
of green fabric ● 16 ×
11in piece of batting

Beautifully Placed

Homemade placemats FEATURING SEASONAL COLORS AND MOTIFS WILL MAKE YOUR MEALS SPECIAL THROUGHOUT THE HOLIDAY SEASON. EACH DESIGN INVOLVES EITHER PATCHWORK OR APPLIQUÉ, PLUS QUILTING. THE PATCHWORK CAN BE SEWN BY HAND OR MACHINE.

COMPLETING THE PLACEMAT

1 *With right sides together, stitch the borders to the left and right sides of the pieced star.*

4 *Fold the two long binding strips in half lengthwise, wrong sides facing, and press.*

5 *Join a red triangle and a green triangle to form a square; repeat to make two squares in all. Now join a patterned triangle and a green triangle; repeat to make two squares in total.*

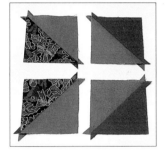

5 *Join a red/green square and a patterned/green square to form a rectangle, with the green triangles on the*

outside. Join the remaining squares in the same way.

6 *Join these two rectangles to form a square, with the green triangles on the outside. This forms the center of the star.*

7 *Join the two rectangles that form the sides of the perimeter to the sides of the square.*

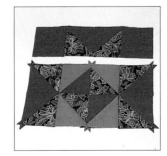

8 *Complete the piecing by adding the remaining strips to the top and bottom edges.*

2 *Sandwich the batting between the patchwork top and the backing fabric, wrong sides facing. Baste through all layers, working from the center outward.*

3 *To quilt the placemat, sew by hand or machine through all three layers around the shapes of the star and border.*

5 *Matching the raw edges and with right sides together, baste the long binding strips to the top and bottom edges of the placemat. Stitch, taking a ¼in seam allowance.*

6 *Turn the binding to the wrong side and hem by hand.*

7 *Use the short strips to bind the side edges in the same way, allowing ½in overlap on each edge and folding this in before turning the binding to the wrong side. Neaten the corners; hem.*

BEAUTIFULLY PLACED

APPLIQUÉ
HOLLY MAT

1 Cut out two pieces of red fabric (one for the top and one for the backing) each piece 16 × 11in.

2 For the binding, cut out two strips of patterned fabric, each 16 × 3in, and two more strips each of which is 12 × 3in.

3 Back the patterned fabric with fusible web, and then cut out the holly leaves from it. Fuse them onto the right side of the top placemat piece.

4 Use a close machine zigzag stitch all around the holly leaves to cover the raw edges.

5 Sandwich the batting between the top and bottom layers and quilt the mat, then bind the edges, as for the Patchwork Star Mat (steps 2-7 of Completing the Placemat).

PATCHWORK MAT
WITH BORDER

1 Make the placemat as for the Appliqué Holly Mat, but instead of steps 3 and 4, substitute a pieced section off-center. The section shown here was worked using Seminole patchwork and features red diamonds with patterned triangles on each side of the diamonds.

APPLIQUÉ BOW
MAT

1 Make the placemat as for the Appliqué Holly Mat, quilting the center, but appliqué bows rather than holly leaves to the corners of the mat.

CENTER OF ATTENTION

CREATE A SPECTACULAR FOCAL POINT FOR YOUR CHRISTMAS TABLE WITH ONE OF THESE BEAUTIFUL CENTERPIECES. (IN FACT, THERE'S NO NEED TO RESTRICT THEM TO THE DINNER TABLE — THEY LOOK GOOD ON ANY TABLE.)

EVERGREEN TRIO

These miniature conifers make an unusual alternative to a traditional table centerpiece.

MATERIALS
3 terracotta plant pots ●
gold spray paint ●
3 small conifers ● moss
● ribbon ● gold tray

1 Spray the plant pots gold, and leave to dry.

2 Transplant the conifers into the pots, covering the soil with a little moss.

3 Tie a ribbon around the base of the stem of each tree, then stand the pots on a gold tray.

ADVENT RING

The candles of Advent rings are traditionally lit on the four Sundays of Advent (one on the first Sunday, two on the second, and so on). Then on Christmas Day the center candle is lit along with the other four.

MATERIALS
Florist's wire ● 5 small potatoes ● circular wire wreath frame ● sphagnum moss ● fine spool wire ● foliage ● 5 white candles (or 1 white candle for the center and 4 red ones)

1 Push a length of florist's wire through each of four potatoes. Scoop a hole out of each to hold the candle. Position them evenly around the ring, and attach by twisting the wire around the frame.

2 Cut a slice off the base of the fifth potato, so it will stand flat. Push two lengths of florist's wire all the way through it at right angles to each other and parallel to the tabletop.

3 Scoop a hole out of the center of the potato for the candle. Fix it into the center of the wreath by twisting the ends of the wires around the frame.

4 Bind moss onto the wreath frame and the cross in the middle using spool wire.

5 Push the stems of the foliage into the moss. Pierce the potatoes with a knitting needle and insert the foliage stems into the holes.

6 Place a tall candle in each potato. Never leave the candles burning unattended, and be sure to replace them before they have burned down too near the foliage.

CENTER OF ATTENTION

TWINKLING LIGHTS

Here, the little candles known as nightlights twinkle among foliage and flowers. The glasses help keep the plant material away from the candles, but make sure none of it strays too near. Never leave them burning unattended.

MATERIALS

Circular wire wreath frame • 6 nightlights in glasses • mossing wire • blocks of green florist's foam • plastic wrap • chicken wire • 2 kinds of foliage • Paper White narcissi • ribbon

1 Shape the wire wreath base into an oval by pulling it out at the sides and pushing it in at the middle.

2 Space the nightlight glasses evenly around the frame, and attach them by winding mossing wire around the nightlights and the frame.

3 Cut the blocks of florist's foam to fit in the gaps between the nightlight glasses. Soak the blocks in water for a minute or two. Wrap them in plastic wrap then in chicken wire.

4 Attach the blocks to the frame by winding wire around them and the frame.

5 Cut short lengths of foliage and push the stems into the foam blocks.

6 Add stems of Paper Whites, using a knitting needle to make holes in the foam for the stems.

7 Wrap ribbon around the outside edge, tying it into a bow.

LONG ON STYLE

This arrangement is an excellent shape for a long table. The stylish container is a silver tranche pan (a shallow rectangular baking pan with a fluted edge).

MATERIALS

Silver tranche pan • green florist's foam • sphagnum moss • ivy • anemones

1 Line the pan with plastic and then fill it with shallow pieces of florist's foam jammed into the shape. Pour water from a pitcher onto the foam until completely saturated.

2 Cover the top of the foam with a fine layer of moss.

FRUIT AND FLOWERS

Kumquat foliage with fruits attached is the basis of this striking arrangement.

MATERIALS
Shallow terracotta plant pot • bronze paint • green florist's foam • sphagnum moss • kumquat foliage with fruits attached • narcissi • ribbon

1 *Spray the pot with bronze paint and leave to dry. Line the pot with plastic.*

2 *Cut florist's foam to fit into it so that it protrudes by about 1½in above the pot. Saturate the foam with water, then cover it with sphagnum moss.*

3 *Cut lengths of foliage, with fruit attached, cutting the stems diagonally to make them pointed. Push them into the foam, arranging them in an even shape.*

4 *Dot narcissi around the shape, using a thick knitting needle to make the holes in the foam for the stems. Finish off with a ribbon tied into a bow.*

3 *Cut diagonally across the stems of ivy leaves to leave short, pointed stems.*

4 *Arrange the ivy all around the edges of the rectangle to make a deep border, first making holes in the foam with a toothpick, then pushing the ivy stems into the holes.*

5 *Cut anemones with short stems. Make holes in the foam for the stems with a thick knitting needle, and dot the anemones among the ivy leaves.*

$\mathscr{S}$EASONAL CHINA

Add a festive touch to the Christmas table by painting border designs onto cheap china with non-toxic ceramic paints or permanent-ink felt-tip pens. Paint on simple patterns using a fine paintbrush (or draw them on with the permanent-ink felt-tip pen). Some ceramic paints are finished, when dry, with a water-based sealer, while others are baked in the oven to set them. Restrict the decoration to the rims of plates or bowls or to items like napkin rings, as neither the paints nor the felt-tip pen should come into contact with food. Save the china for Christmas, and wash it very carefully by hand.

$\mathscr{S}$ETTING THE SCENE

$\mathscr{T}$HE HOLIDAY TABLE CAN LOOK VERY FESTIVE AND SEASONAL WITH-OUT TOO MUCH TIME OR EXPENSE. HERE ARE SOME QUICK AND EASY IDEAS FOR BRINGING CHRISTMAS TO YOUR TABLE.

$\mathscr{N}$APKIN RINGS

Use your ingenuity to make simple but striking napkin rings with a seasonal look.

Decorate a dark green wooden napkin ring using a permanent-ink gold felt-tip pen.

Twine ivy around the napkin, winding a length of cord over the stem and tying the ends together on the underside to hold the ivy in place.

Paint wooden acorns (the type used on roller shades) gold and attach them to both ends of a length of gold cord. Tie the cord around the

napkin, finishing off with a single ivy leaf tucked into it.

ALMOST INSTANT PLACEMATS

Add seasonal decorations to thin cakeboards or cardboard circles about 12in in diameter.

- Cover them with colored corrugated cardboard, glued in place. Make holes around the rim at regular intervals then wind ribbon through the holes, tying the ends in a bow.

- Glue gold cardboard over the circles, then glue gold-painted bay leaves around the rim. Arrange the leaves so they point toward the top on each side, starting with the smallest leaves at the top and getting bigger toward the bottom, like a Roman crown. Finish the base with a taffeta bow.

Glue two bay leaves and a small pine cone painted gold onto a wooden napkin ring. Finish with a bow of red and gold cord.

Wind gold paper around the napkin, then tie with a wire-edged crimson and gold ribbon.

Use a tin star cookie cutter with glass "jewels" glued to each side surface.

DISTINCTIVE PLACE CARDS

Make your table distinctive with really special name cards.

Make an ivy "topiary tree" for each guest. Pack pieces of florist's foam into small terracotta pots. Cut an old wooden broom handle into 7in lengths, cutting the ends diagonally into points. For each tree, push one end into the foam in the pot, and the other into a florist's foam ball or cone. Spray the pot and stick gold. Cover the foam with sphagnum moss held in place with 1¼in lengths of florist's wire bent into "U" shapes. Wind lengths of ivy over the moss and attach in the same way. Cover the top of the pot with more moss. Attach card labels with a cord bow using florist's wire.

GOING WITH A BANG

An English Christmas table isn't complete without traditional Christmas firecrackers, and here's how to make some for your holiday table. They are sure to make Christmas dinner go with a bang!

MATERIALS

Crepe paper • tracing paper • stick adhesive, clear adhesive • foil wrapping paper • thin cardboard • twine

FOR EACH CRACKER

Cracker snap (available from some craft stores) • gift • motto • paper hat • decoration

1 *For one cracker, cut out a 6¼ × 13¾in rectangle from crepe paper, cutting so that the longest sides are parallel to the straight grain of the crepe paper.*

2 *Cut out a 6 × 13½in rectangle from tracing paper. Apply two lines of stick adhesive on the tracing paper, each parallel to a short edge and 4in in from it.*

3 *Position the tracing paper on the crepe paper, leaving a narrow border all around, so the papers stick together along the glue lines.*

4 *Cut two 4 × 6¼in rectangles from foil wrapping paper, trimming along the longer sides with pinking shears.*

5 *Use stick adhesive to glue the foil pieces to the crepe paper so the pinked foil edges are parallel to the shorter edges of the crepe paper and 2in in. The other edges of the foil and crepe paper should be even.*

6 *Cut two 6 × 8¼in rectangles from thin cardboard. Roll these rectangles up to make two 8¼in-long tubes.*

7 Overlap the edges of the two tubes by about ½in and stick them together with clear adhesive. These will be reused to make all the crackers.

8 For each cracker, cut a 6 × 4¾in rectangle from thin cardboard. Roll it up into a 4¼in-long tube and glue the edges, as in steps 6 and 7.

9 Place the three cardboard tubes end to end on the tracing paper, positioning them centrally. Lay a cracker snap next to them, so the center of the snap is level with that of the shorter tube.

10 Apply a thin line of clear glue along one long edge of the paper. Then, beginning at the opposite edge, roll up the cracker toward the glued edge. Overlap the long edges, and leave till dry.

11 Pull out one of the longer tubes by 2in. Crimp the foil by wrapping twine around the center of the foil and pulling the ends tightly while holding them at right angles to the cracker.

12 Remove the foil and twine. Drop the gifts into the cracker through the other end. Pull out the remaining long cardboard tube slightly, and crimp the foil as in step 11.

13 Remove this cardboard tube and the twine, and glue a decoration onto the cracker.

14 To pull the cracker, two people each hold one end of the cracker snap down with their thumb, grasping the crimped portion of the cracker between two fingers, then they pull in opposite directions.

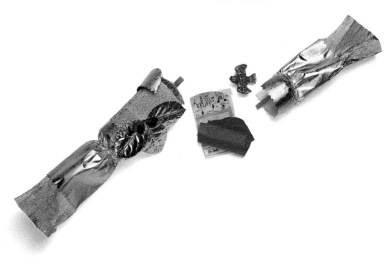

GOOD ENOUGH TO EAT

CHILDREN WILL ADORE A TREE TRIMMED WITH EDIBLE DECORATIONS. THE PROBLEM WILL NOT BE MAKING THE DECORATIONS — WHICH ARE ALL VERY EASY TO DO — BUT KEEPING THE TREE FULLY DECORATED!

FRUIT AND NUTS

Fruit and nuts can easily be turned into decorative tree ornaments. Just glue a loop of ribbon or gold cord to whole nuts, and tie thin gold cord around kumquats or tangerines. Another idea (not illustrated) is to thread slices of candied fruits with gold wire for hanging.

CHRISTMAS COOKIES

No selection of edible decorations would be complete without Christmas cookies. Here's a recipe that makes about 25–30 cookies.

[1] Combine 8oz sifted all-purpose flour with 4oz dark brown sugar (or granulated sugar for a paler cookie). Rub in ¼ cup butter.

[2] Stir in one beaten egg and mix well.

[3] Dissolve ¾ teaspoon baking soda in 2 teaspoons warm water. Add this to the flour mixture and mix till you have a pliable dough. Add a drop of milk if necessary.

[4] Roll out on a floured board to a thickness of ⅛ in. Cut out all kinds of shapes, for example, stars, moons, birds, angels, rings, hearts, fish and bells.

[5] Using a small metal icing tube, make holes for hanging.

[6] Place on greased baking sheets and bake in a preheated oven at 350°F for about 15 minutes, or until the cookies are just beginning to brown.

[7] Remove from the baking sheet and enlarge the holes if necessary while still warm. Cool on a rack.

[8] When cool, pipe icing designs, or frost with a mixture of confectioner's sugar and a little egg white to give a frosty glaze.

[9] Hang the cookies on the tree with ribbons or gold cord threaded through the holes.

CANDY CHAINS

Pieces of candy in plain, shiny wrappings can be made into colorful chains by wiring or tying them to a long length of thin ribbon or cord.

GOODY BAGS

Make small bundles of cellophane containing sugared almonds, fudge, wrapped candy, dried fruits, or nuts. Tie them with ribbon or gold cord and hang from the tree.

POPCORN GARLANDS

Traditional popcorn garlands look sensational. All you do is thread the popped corn onto strong thread to form long garlands, then drape them over the tree. For a more colorful version, alternate fresh cranberries with the popcorn; they should last for about two weeks.

POPCORN BALLS

Popcorn can also be used for balls. To make them, prepare a syrup from 2 tablespoons each of butter and light brown sugar and 5oz marshmallows. Add 7½ cups popped corn, and stir well. Then, with wet hands, mold the mixture into small ball shapes and leave to set on waxed paper. When cold, tie the popcorn balls with gold cord or ribbon and hang from the tree.

TINY BASKETS

Little baskets containing candy look pretty hanging among the fir branches.

CHAPTER SIX

CHRISTMAS KEEPSAKES

For many people the holiday only begins when the box of Christmas decorations is brought out, and well-loved items are carefully unwrapped and restored to their once-a-year places. This treasure trove is even more valued if some of the decorations have been handmade, providing reminders of past Christmases and evenings of shared enjoyment. Making your own decorations is a way of reviving the spirit of a traditional Christmas, and working on them is all the more enjoyable when you know they will be used for many Christmases to come.

Christmas Keepsakes

All the projects in this chapter can be made by complete beginners in craftwork. Some involve a few specialist techniques and tools, but the techniques are quickly learned, and if you have never tackled the particular craft before you will have the satisfaction of mastering new skills.

Candles have always been associated with Christmas, and in pre-Christian days with pagan midwinter festivals. Candlemaking is itself a traditional Christmas craft, and also a rewarding one. Groups of candles look very festive and create a wonderfully cozy, intimate atmosphere, whether used at the dinner table, placed on a mantelpiece, or grouped around a room. They are not hard to make, and in this chapter you'll find a varied selection of candles to make or decorate yourself, as well as ideas for displaying them.

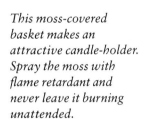

This moss-covered basket makes an attractive candle-holder. Spray the moss with flame retardant and never leave it burning unattended.

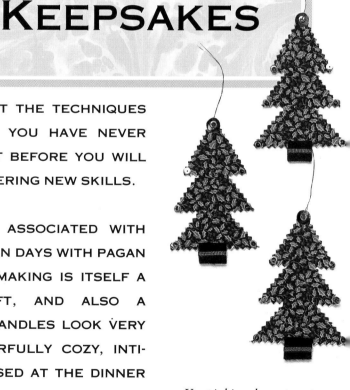

Use pinking shears to cut these trees from two pieces of fabric bonded together with fusible web (see page 134 for pattern). Glue on sequins and felt pots trimmed with braid.

ANOTHER KITCHEN CRAFT, LESS TRADITIONAL THAN CANDLEMAKING BUT INCREASINGLY POPULAR, IS DOUGH SCULPTURE. BREAD DOUGH MADE WITH A HIGH PROPORTION OF SALT, THEN BAKED AND DECORATED, WILL LAST INDEFINITELY AND IS REMARKABLY VERSATILE. IT CAN BE USED FOR A WIDE VARIETY OF DECORATIONS, INCLUDING CHRISTMAS TREE ORNAMENTS AND WREATHS.

This basket of fruit is built up from small hand-modeled pieces of dough (see pages 124–5). Roll balls for the fruit and weave the basket from long pieces. Omit wallpaper paste from the recipe and add 1 tablespoon of vegetable oil.

"TREES" MADE FROM PINE CONES OR RIBBONS LOOK SPECTACULAR AND CONTRAST PLEASINGLY WITH CHRISTMAS GREENERY. OUR TWO ARE BOTH SURPRISINGLY EASY TO MAKE, AS IS THE CHRISTMAS MOBILE. ANOTHER TYPE OF DECORATION THAT MAKES A COMPLETE CHANGE FROM EVERGREENS, THIS IS MADE UP FROM DELICATE HANGINGS, AND CAN BE SEEN TO BEST ADVANTAGE HUNG IN FRONT OF A WINDOW OR DANGLING FROM A BARE BRANCH.

WOODWORKING MAY SOUND A DAUNTING PROSPECT, BUT THE CHUNKY WOODEN CHRISTMAS TREES WILL GIVE DRAMATIC RESULTS EVEN IF YOU ARE A TOTAL BEGINNER, AND LOOK VERY PERKY AND COLORFUL GROUPED TOGETHER. THE FOLK-ART ANGEL GABRIEL IS MORE DIFFICULT, BUT A GREAT CHANCE TO TRY YOUR HAND AT THE PAINT TECHNIQUE KNOWN AS "ANTIQUING" — IT IS, AFTER ALL, AN HEIRLOOM YOU ARE MAKING!

GENERAL WORKBOX
see page 7

WOODWORKING WORKBOX
rasp • file • coping saw • backsaw • drill • craft knife • fine sandpaper

CANDLEMAKING WORKBOX
wax or sugar thermometer (optional) • scissors • paper towels • craft knife

DOUGH-CRAFT WORKBOX
mixing bowl • fork • rolling pin • non-stick baking parchment • plastic wrap • skewer (optional) • aluminum foil (optional)

A variation of the Ribbon Tree on page 116, this tree is covered entirely in loops of ribbon.

EVERLASTING TREES

*H*ERE ARE TWO TREES THAT YOU CAN BRING OUT AT THE BEGIN-NING OF THE HOLIDAY SEASON FULLY DE-CORATED AND READY TO ADD CHRISTMAS CHEER TO YOUR HOME.

*R*IBBON TREE

MATERIALS

5in Styrofoam® ball ● 12in wooden dowel or squared wood trim, for stem ● basket ● ready-to-mix cement ● selection of ribbons in different colors and widths: here, ¼in, 2¾in, ⅝in, ⅜in, ⅞in: approximately 6½yd of each ● florist's spool wire ● 16 gold-sprayed dried poppy heads ● 16 small bunches of artificial gold berries ● 16 gold filigree plastic leaves ● reindeer moss

1 Spear the Styrofoam ball on the dowel and set the dowel in cement in the plant pot as for the Cone Tree, steps 1–4.

2 Cut the 2¾in-wide ribbon in half length-wise. Cut some of this divided ribbon into 15 lengths, each 7in long. Double up the ribbon to form a single-loop bow. Twist wire around the center, leaving one long end.

3 Cut the remaining divided ribbon and all the other ribbon into 15in lengths. Make double-loop bows.

4 Twist wires around the bunches of berries, the gold leaves, and the poppy heads.

5 Set aside two poppy heads, one bunch of berries, three gold leaves, and two ribbon bows.

6 Stud the ball with the remaining loop bows, alternating them with the poppy heads and berries and distributing colors evenly. Ensure each is firmly set into the ball.

7 When the ball is completely covered, insert the wired gold leaves into the ball, interspersing them among the ribbons.

8 Tease the reindeer moss out gently so that it lies naturally around the base of the tree.

9 Group the reserved poppy heads, leaves, berries, and loops. Glue them lightly to one side of the basket.

CONE TREE

MATERIALS

Florist's foam cone, about 11in high • 7in length of ½in squared wood trim or dowel • ready-to-mix cement • plant pot about 4in in diameter and 4in high • spray paint • about 50 small pine cones • florist's wire • small block dry florist's foam • variety of seeds, such as mustard, caraway, sesame, cardamom, peppercorns • gold braid • fresh bay leaves

1 Spear the florist's foam cone on the length of wood, allowing about 4in of the wood to protrude from the base. Remove the wood.

2 Mix up enough cement to almost fill the plant pot, and pour it into the pot. Stick the length of wood in the center, securing it with a web of masking tape across the top of the pot.

3 When the cement has set (after about 24 hours), spray-paint the pot and the length of wood. Leave to dry.

4 Apply glue to the length of wood and slot the foam cone onto it as before.

5 Wire the pine cones by looping florist's wire between the petals at the base of the cone then twisting the wire back on itself.

6 Cut about 20 small shapes such as wedges, balls, and pyramids from the block of florist's foam. Cover with glue and press on the seeds.

7 Insert a short length of wire into each seed-covered shape. Wrap gold braid around some shapes.

8 Insert the wires of the pine cones and seed-covered shapes into the foam cone till the foam is completely covered. Try to have larger cones at the bottom, and distribute the seed-covered shapes evenly.

9 Insert the stems of fresh bay leaves into the cone. Replace each year.

CANDLE POWER

FOR CREATING ATMOSPHERE, CANDLES ARE UN-SURPASSED. YOU CAN USE BOUGHT CANDLES IN IMAGINATIVE ARRANGEMENTS OR YOU CAN MAKE YOUR OWN AT HOME. HERE, BEESWAX CANDLES AND TERRACOTTA POTS PROVIDE THE BASICS AND YOU CAN LET YOUR IMAGINATION RUN RIOT ON THE DECORATION. HOWEVER, ALWAYS REMEMBER THAT CANDLES CAN BE DANGEROUS. SPRAY INFLAMMABLE MATERIALS WITH FLAME RETARDANT, PLACE CANDLES ON METAL OR FOIL TRAYS, AND NEVER LEAVE THEM UNATTENDED.

CANDLE POWER

MATERIALS

ALL HOMEMADE CANDLES
Suitable molds (see method) • candle wax • candle-making dyes • candle wicks 2in longer than height of mold

MOSAIC CANDLE
Odd pieces of colored candles

HONEYCOMB CANDLE
Mold seal or modeling clay (optional)

- Buy flexible or rigid candle molds, or improvise your own. Anything that will withstand boiling water – such as glazed pottery, glass, metal, and some plastic – is suitable.

 Unless the mold can be broken or cut away, it should be slightly wider at the top, with no obstructions that would stop the candle from being removed.

- To prevent cracking, glass molds should be warmed with very hot water before being filled with wax.

DECORATED CANDLES
Bought candles • poster paints • small sponge • sequins • glass-headed pins • glitter • silver paint • star stickers

- You can give bought candles – or simple homemade ones – a seasonal touch with applied decoration.

- Decorate bought white candles by sponging with poster paints. Pour a little paint into a saucer, and dip a small sponge (a natural one will give the best effect) into it. Press onto a paper towel to remove excess paint, then dab all over the candle. Leave to dry before applying a second color.

- Brighten up ordinary candles by gluing sequins, glitter, or star stickers all over them. Or pin sequins on with glass-headed pins. Alternatively, gently melt the surface with a hair-dryer then press sequins or glitter in place.

- Create a sgraffito effect by carving out shapes on the candle with a craft knife, then painting the carved lines with silver paint.

LAYERED CANDLE

1 *Tie the wick to a small metal weight such as a washer. Tie the other end to a metal rod, nail, or pencil. Support the rod across the top of the mold, so the weight barely touches the base.*

2 *Break the wax into small pieces and put it into pans (never cans, as wax can leak through the soldered seams), one for each color. Add dye.*

3 *Very gently heat the color that will be the bottom stripe, stirring until the dye dissolves. Do not leave it unattended while it is heating.*

4 *Remove from the heat and allow it to cool slightly. If you have a wax or sugar thermometer, the wax should be at a temperature of 180°F. Pour it into the mold. Place the mold in cold water.*

5 *For slanting layers, support the mold in a tilted position. (First fix the wick centrally by pouring in a little wax and allowing it to set before adding the rest of the first layer.)*

6 *Allow the wax to partially set. Do not leave it to harden completely or the layers will not fuse together. However, if you pour in the next layer when the first is too liquid, they will simply blend.*

7 *Once a good skin has formed on the wax, heat the next color and pour it on. Leave to partially set. Repeat until the mold is filled with different layers. Leave to harden completely.*

8 *As the wax cools, it will shrink and a well may form at the top, so add a little more melted wax as necessary to keep the top level.*

9 *Remove the candle from the mold and cut off the surplus wick, leaving about ½in.*

10 *To give your candle an attractive shine, polish it with a cloth and a tiny dab of cooking oil. How smooth and shiny the inside of the mold is also affects how shiny the candle is.*

HONEYCOMB CANDLE

Filling the mold with ice before adding wax creates an attractive honeycomb texture when the ice melts. However, the wick must be prevented from absorbing water or the flame could splutter.

1 *To do this, dip the wick in hot wax before fixing it in place, as for the Layered Candle, step 1.*

2 *Alternatively, use a candle as the core. It should be ½in shorter than the mold, thread the wick through a hole in the base. Seal the hole with mold seal or modeling clay.*

3 *Pack ice around the wick or candle – the size will determine the texture. Crushed ice will produce a lacy effect.*

4 *Fill the mold with wax, pouring slowly so it fills all the spaces around the ice. Leave to set, then carefully unmold.*

SHELL CANDLES

Shell candles look beautiful in a group. Beach-collect shells with fairly flat bases, or buy common, non- endangered shells. Fix the wick to the base of the shell with a little florist's putty and pour wax into the shell. Leave to cool.

SCENTED CANDLES

To create scented candles, simply add a few drops of aromatic essential oil to the hot wax just before pouring it into the mold.

MOSAIC CANDLE

1 *Put the wick in the mold as for the Layered Candle, step 1. Loosely fill the mold with small chunks of candles in different colors.*

2 *Make sure that the candle chunks are pressed firmly against the side of the mold and that the wick is not dislodged from the center.*

3 *Heat some wax with a light-colored dye as for the Layered Candle, steps 2-4. Pour it into the mold when it is about 160°F.*

4 *Put the mold in a pan of cold water. Leave to harden, then unmold.*

CHUNKY WOODEN TREES

MATERIALS

BASIC TREE

*1in- thick pine: 6 × 8in
piece for each tree •
non-toxic craft paints •
gold or silver pen
(optional)*

TREE WITH CANDLES

¼in dowel

PATTERN PAGE 139

BASIC TREE

1 *Transfer the pattern
to the piece of wood. Cut
out the tree shape using a
coping saw. Rub with
fine sandpaper for a
smooth finish.*

2 *Paint the tree green,
the trunk brown, and the
pot red or brown. If
desired, use red paint or
silver or gold pen to add
bows and balls.*

3 *The snow effect is
created by first masking
the base with masking
tape, then loading an old
toothbrush with white
paint and flicking your
thumb across the top to
spatter it.*

TREE WITH CANDLES

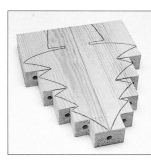

1 *Transfer the pattern
to the pine. Mark out
steps at the sides, and
then cut the steps using a
backsaw.*

2 *In each step drill a
¼in hole for the
"candle."*

3 *Finish cutting the
outline of the tree with
the coping saw.*

4 *Use a craft knife to
carve a candle flame on
the end of a piece of
dowel (like sharpening a
pencil with a knife). The
dowel should be about
2ft long so you have
something to hold while
carving.*

FESTIVE FOLK ART

5 *After carving, cut it
to the required length.
Repeat for the other
candles.*

6 *Paint the tree as for
the Basic Tree, steps 2
and 3. Paint the candles
separately. When dry
glue them into the holes.*

ANGEL GABRIEL

MATERIALS

*1in-thick pine: 8 × 20in
• sponge • soft cloth •
sand-sealer • gesso •
small pot of sienna (or
any other reddish) oil
paint • small pot gold-
size • bronzing powder
(here light gold 100) •
small tubes of artist's
oils (here burnt sienna
and raw umber) •
mineral spirits •
transparent oil glaze •
semi-gloss varnish •
crackle varnish •
hairdryer (optional)*

1 *Transfer the pattern to the piece of pine. Use a coping saw to cut around the outer edge, taking particular care with the angel's face and hands.*

2 *Drill a ¼in hole through each of the two areas to be cut out (between the arm and the horn, and between the sash and the body). Introduce the coping saw blade through these holes and carefully cut out.*

3 *Create 3-D effects with a rasp, file, and craft knife. Rub over with fine sandpaper for a smooth finish ready to paint.*

4 *Wipe the angel with a damp sponge to remove any dust and to raise the grain. Allow to dry. Sand with finer sandpaper. Apply sand-sealer. Allow to dry.*

5 *Apply gesso. Allow to dry. Sand with very fine sandpaper until the surface is very smooth.*

6 *Apply sienna oil paint to all areas that are to be gilded. Allow to dry. Apply gold-size.*

7 *When the size goes sticky, apply bronzing powder. (Wear a mask while dusting.) Allow to dry. Gently remove any excess bronzing powder with a soft cloth.*

8 *Make up an antique glaze using equal parts burnt sienna and mineral spirits. Mix with equal parts transparent oil glaze. Paint the angel and then rub over with a soft cloth. This will remove any excess mixture.*

9 *Load your brush with the mixture and run your thumb across it, so the mixture spatters over the angel.*

10 *Blot the spatter with a soft cloth to smudge the spots, making them more irregular. Allow to dry.*

11 *Apply semi-gloss varnish. When it is almost dry, apply a coat of crackle varnish. If you want fine cracks, let it dry naturally. If you want a stronger crackle effect, use a hairdryer. Do not hold it too close or you could scorch the wood.*

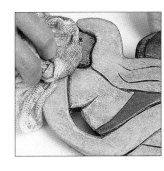

12 *Apply a second antique glaze made from equal parts raw umber and mineral spirits. Gently wipe off with soft cloth, making sure the glaze goes into the cracks. Allow to dry.*

HOLLY WREATH

This holly wreath, like all dough "sculptures," is built up from small pieces. Flat shapes like these leaves are the easiest. A high-gloss varnish has been used here, but other designs might look better with a satin finish.

MATERIALS

2 cups all-purpose flour • 1 cup salt • 2 tablespoons wallpaper paste • water • cookie cutter in holly-leaf shape • poster paints • felt-tip pen (optional) • varnish

1 Combine the salt, flour, and wallpaper paste. Add water gradually, mixing first with a fork and then with your hand, until the dough is stiff but not sticky.

2 Turn the dough out onto a work surface and knead for about ten minutes, until smooth.

3 To prevent the dough from drying out, keep it wrapped in plastic until you are ready to use it.

On a lightly floured surface, roll out the dough to a thickness of ¼in.

4 Cut out the wreath shape using a 9½in plate and a 6in plate as patterns.

5 Lift the ring carefully onto a baking sheet lined with non-stick baking parchment.

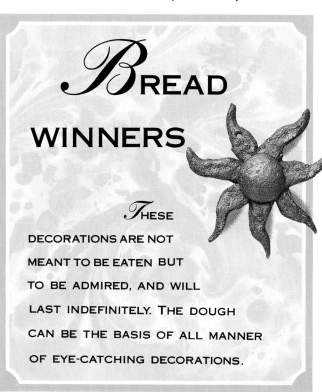

BREAD WINNERS

THESE DECORATIONS ARE NOT MEANT TO BE EATEN BUT TO BE ADMIRED, AND WILL LAST INDEFINITELY. THE DOUGH CAN BE THE BASIS OF ALL MANNER OF EYE-CATCHING DECORATIONS.

6 Make a ball of the remaining dough and roll out again. Use a holly cutter to make leaf shapes. Mark the leaf veins with a knife.

7 Moisten the holly leaves with water and position them on the wreath, overlapping the ends. The water will secure them. Make a hole at the top of the wreath for hanging.

8 Form berries from small pieces of dough, and attach them in the same way. (Any leftover dough can be wrapped in plastic and stored in the refrigerator for up to a week.)

9 Bake the wreath at 225°F. for approximately eight hours until it is dry. Leave to cool.

10 Decorate with poster paints, adding shading and highlights if desired

Natural Wreath

You can create a very different effect by leaving the wreath unpainted.

MATERIALS

2 cups wholewheat flour
• 1 cup salt •
4 tablespoons wallpaper paste • cookie cutter •
egg or condensed milk •
varnish

1 For a textured finish, use wholewheat rather than white flour, and increase the amount of wallpaper paste by two tablespoons.

2 Create a golden-brown finish by brushing the wreath with egg white or yolk or condensed milk before baking. Varnish both sides, perhaps with a satin-finish varnish.

to prevent the leaves from looking too flat. Felt-tip pen is useful for detail.

11 Once the paint is dry, varnish both sides of the wreath twice. (If you do this before the paint is completely dry, the colors may run.)

Tree Decorations

This bread-dough technique lends itself well to Christmas tree decorations.

MATERIALS

Dough • paints •
varnish • cookie cutters
• ribbon • assorted
trimmings (optional)

1 Cut out simple shapes like stars, bells, trees, and holly with cookie cutters, or use a pattern and a sharp knife.

2 For the more elaborate shapes, such as

the toy soldiers, trace around Christmas card or book illustrations. Make sure areas like the neck are not too thin or they could break.

3 Simple shapes such as the star, sun, and moon can be formed by hand.

4 For all tree ornaments, you will need to make a hanging hole at the top with a skewer before baking at 225°F until completely dry.

5 Prior to baking, you can add detail by sticking on extra bits of dough to make raised edges, fur trim, etc. This will prevent the shapes from looking too flat.

6 To create a three-dimensional dome shape, support flat pieces on crumpled foil while baking.

7 For a stained-glass effect, cut out small squares and circles in the dough. After baking, glue colored tissue paper behind them.

8 Another idea is to make indentations in the dough and then glue glass "jewels" into them after baking.

9 For a sparkly effect, dip the varnished pieces in glitter before the varnish has dried.

10 After varnishing, the ornaments can be decorated with ribbons, braid, sequins, or other trimming.

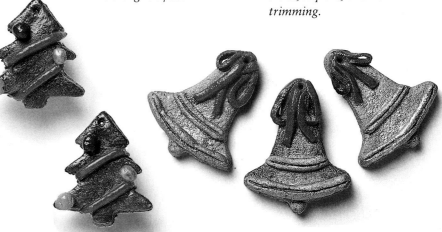

CHRISTMAS MOBILES

*D*ELICATE MOBILES MAKE BEAUTIFUL DECORATIONS LIGHTLY FLUTTERING AT A WINDOW. THESE PRETTY MOBILES, MADE FROM A VARIETY OF UNUSUAL MATERIALS, WOULD LOOK EQUALLY STUNNING ON THE TREE.

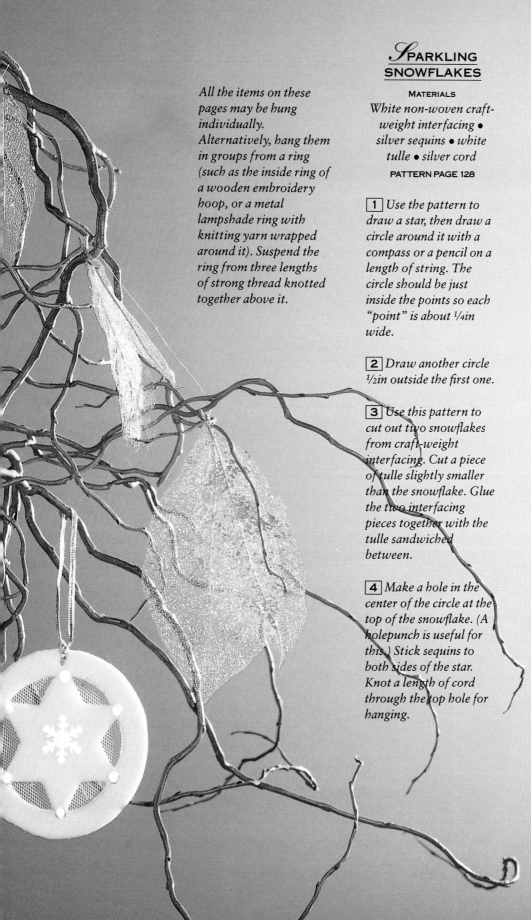

All the items on these pages may be hung individually. Alternatively, hang them in groups from a ring (such as the inside ring of a wooden embroidery hoop, or a metal lampshade ring with knitting yarn wrapped around it). Suspend the ring from three lengths of strong thread knotted together above it.

SPARKLING SNOWFLAKES

MATERIALS

White non-woven craft-weight interfacing • silver sequins • white tulle • silver cord

PATTERN PAGE 128

1 Use the pattern to draw a star, then draw a circle around it with a compass or a pencil on a length of string. The circle should be just inside the points so each "point" is about ¼in wide.

2 Draw another circle ½in outside the first one.

3 Use this pattern to cut out two snowflakes from craft-weight interfacing. Cut a piece of tulle slightly smaller than the snowflake. Glue the two interfacing pieces together with the tulle sandwiched between.

4 Make a hole in the center of the circle at the top of the snowflake. (A holepunch is useful for this.) Stick sequins to both sides of the star. Knot a length of cord through the top hole for hanging.

JEWELED STARS

MATERIALS

Sequin waste in different colors • 1in sequins • ½in glass "jewels" • fine cord

PATTERN PAGE 128

1 Use the pattern to cut out from sequin waste one star shape in one color and two in a second color.

2 Sandwich the single star shape between the two that are in the second color.

3 Glue a sequin to the center of each side of the star so they stick together, then glue a glass "jewel" to the center of each sequin. Knot cord through the sequin waste ready for hanging.

COLORFUL RINGS

MATERIALS

Synthetic raffia • ribbon roses • 2in curtain rings • fine cord

1 Cut a 60in length of synthetic raffia. Tucking under the end, wind it around and around the curtain ring. Knot the other end around the screw eye.

2 Glue a ribbon rose to each side of the screw eye. Thread cord through the screw eye; knot it, ready for hanging.

LEAF FILIGREE

MATERIALS

Green leaves (here, magnolia) • gold or silver spray paint • small paintbrush • fine gold or silver thread

1 Soak green leaves (not dry or brown) in a bucket of rainwater for about a month. Soak more than you will need, as they tear easily.

2 Take the leaves out of the bucket and use a fine paintbrush to carefully remove the leaf from the skeleton.

3 Spray the skeleton leaves with paint. When dry, thread with matching sewing thread ready for hanging.

PATTERNS

GENERAL SHAPE — BOW

PATTERNS SHOWN ON LARGE GRIDS ARE LIFE-SIZE; PATTERNS SHOWN ON THE SMALL GRIDS SHOULD BE ENLARGED TO TWICE THE SIZE. IF YOU HAVE ACCESS TO A PHOTOCOPIER WITH AN ENLARGING FACILITY, SIMPLY SET IT TO 200%. OTHERWISE, DRAW UP YOUR OWN GRID, MAKING THE SQUARES ¾IN, AND COPY THE SHAPES ONTO YOUR NEW GRID, SQUARE BY SQUARE, USING THE GRID PATTERNS IN THE BOOK AS A GUIDE.

GENERAL SHAPE — CANDLES

FIVE-POINTED STAR

SIX-POINTED STAR

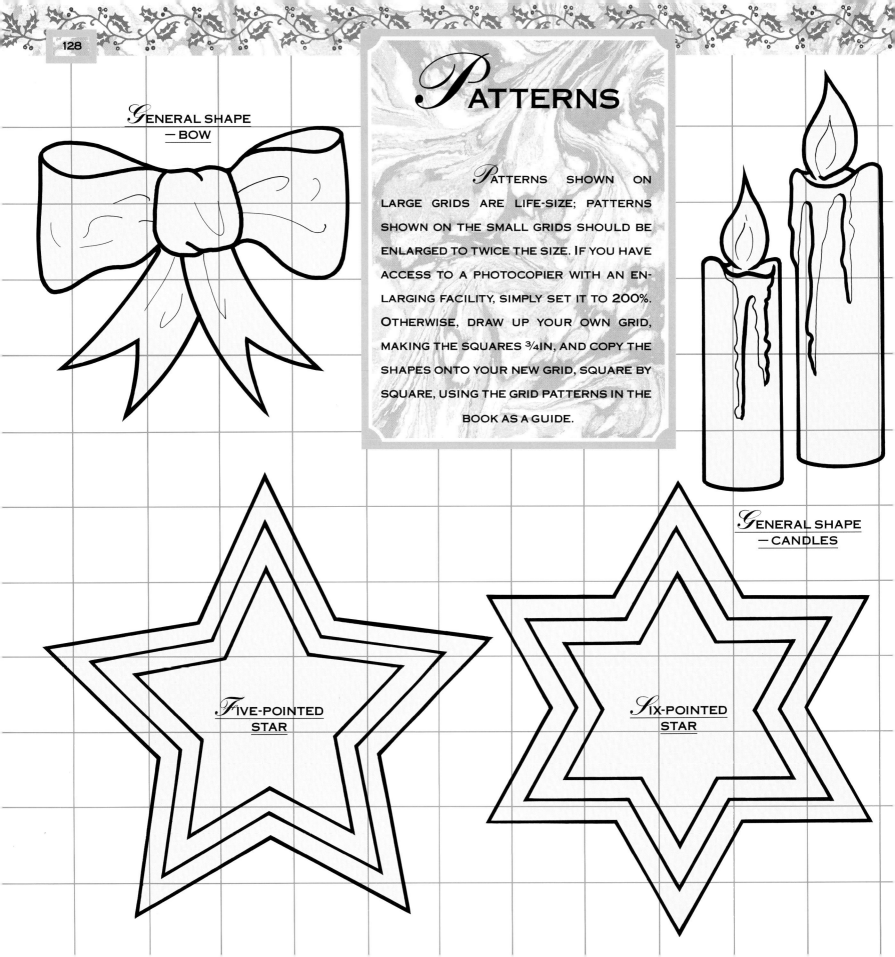

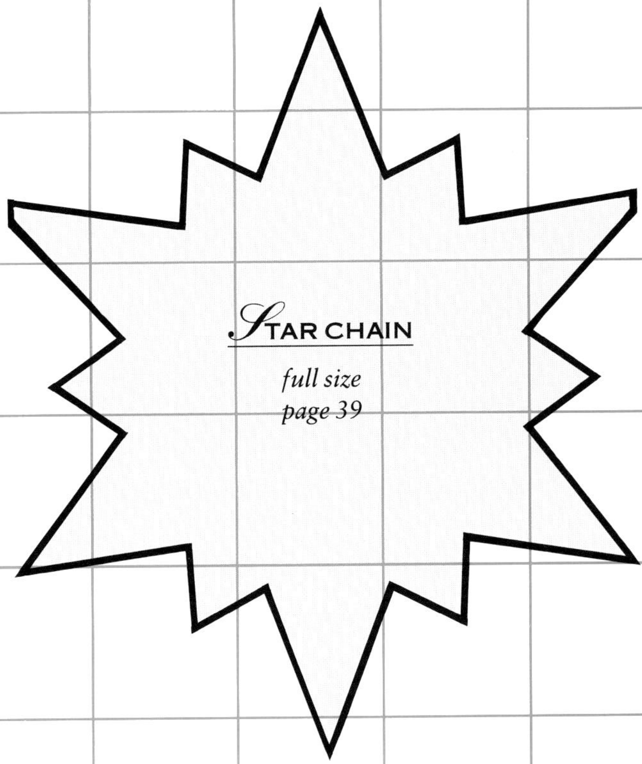

STAR CHAIN

*full size
page 39*

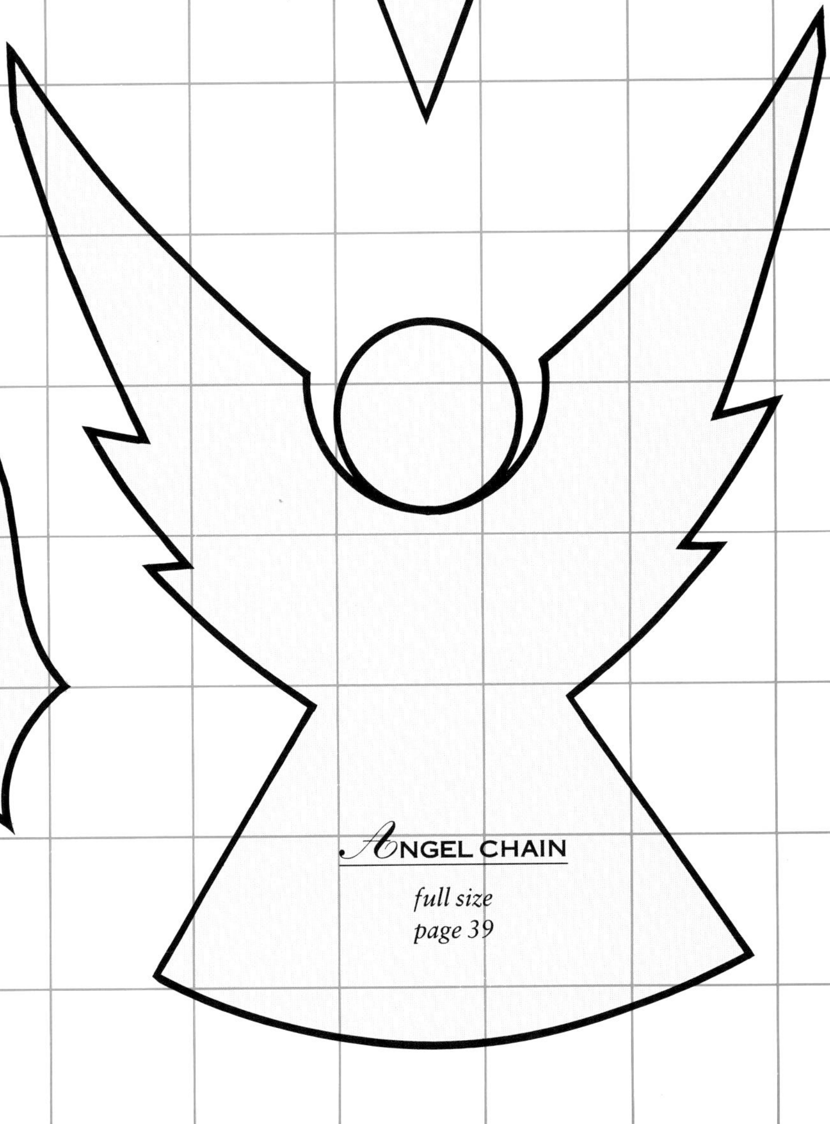

**GENERAL SHAPE
— BELLS**

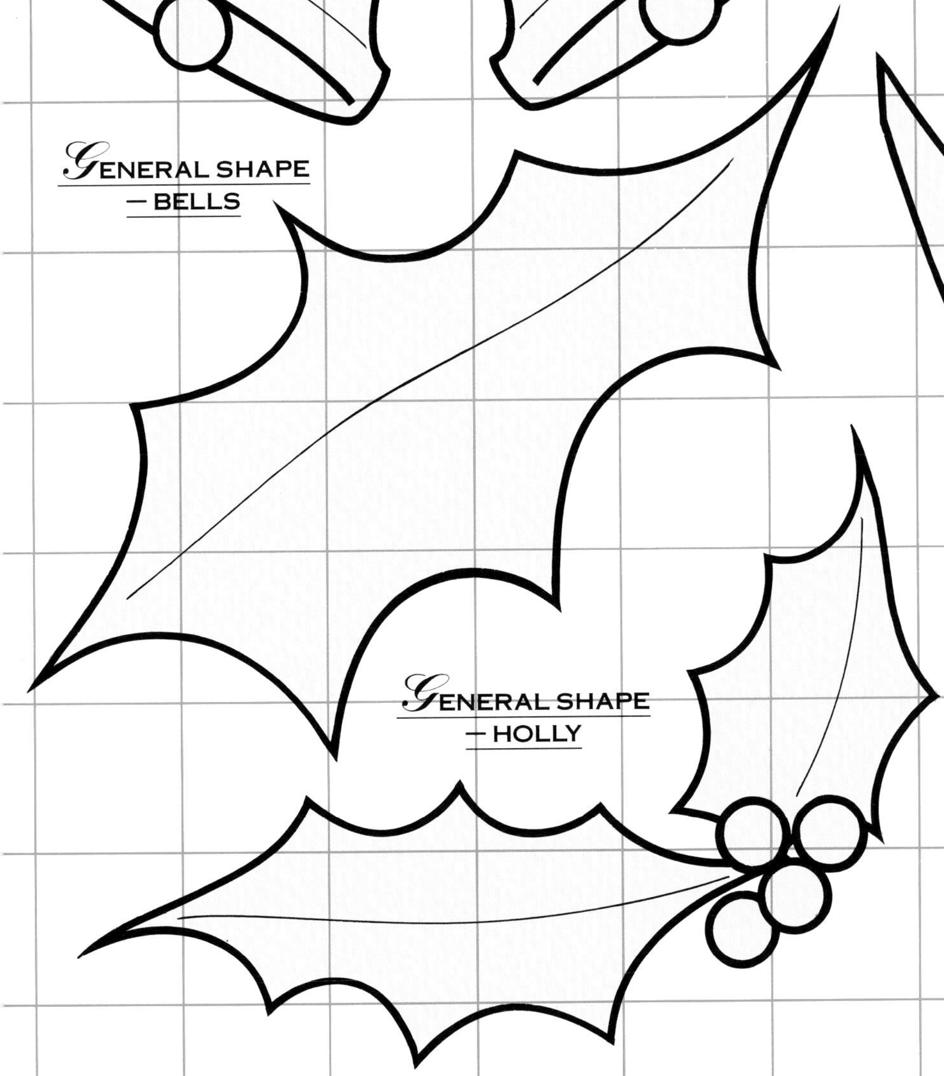

**GENERAL SHAPE
— HOLLY**

ANGEL CHAIN

*full size
page 39*

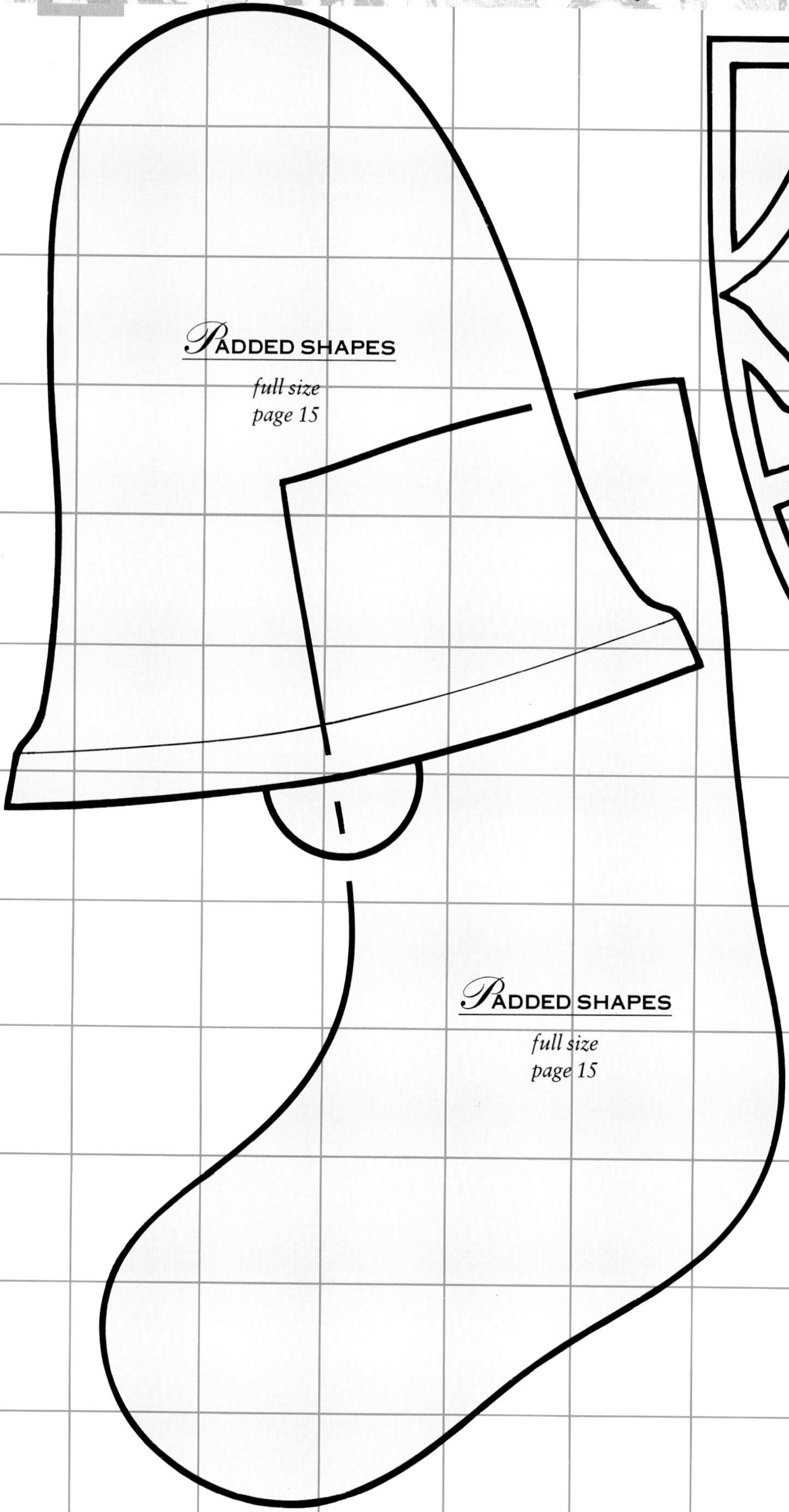

*P*ADDED SHAPES

full size
page 15

*S*TENCILED
WINDOW

full size
page 12

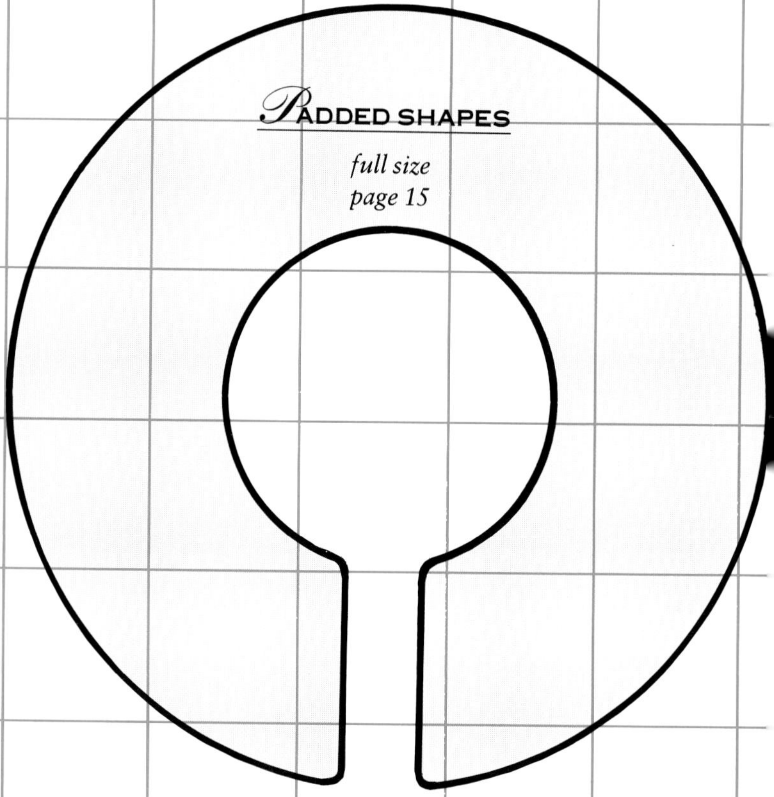

*P*ADDED SHAPES

full size
page 15

*P*ADDED SHAPES

full size
page 15

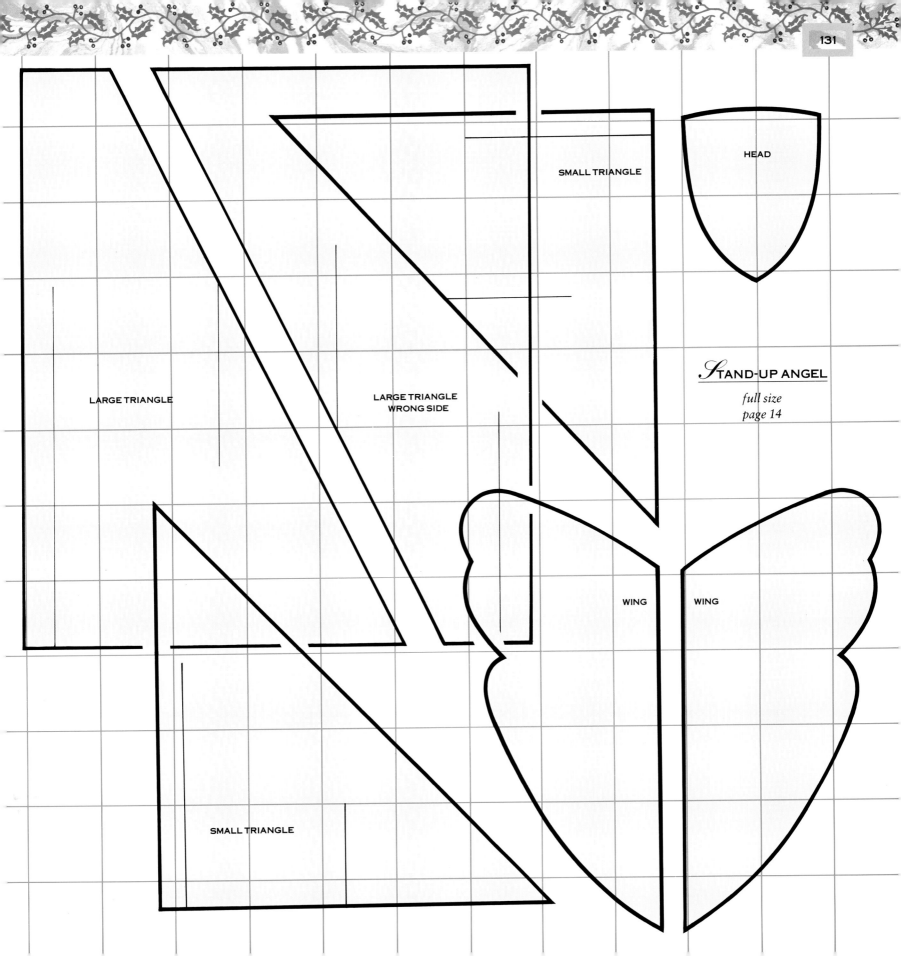

LARGE TRIANGLE

LARGE TRIANGLE
WRONG SIDE

SMALL TRIANGLE

SMALL TRIANGLE

HEAD

WING   WING

*S*TAND-UP ANGEL

full size
page 14

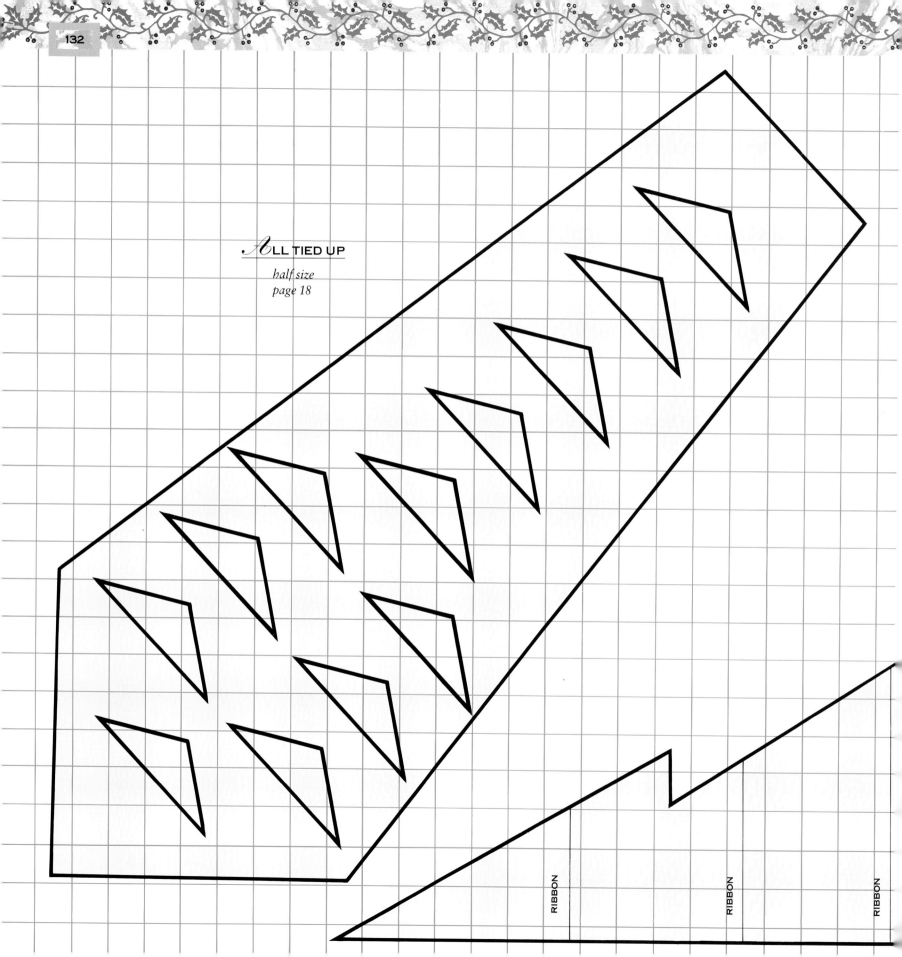

*A*LL TIED UP

half size
page 18

RIBBON

RIBBON

RIBBON

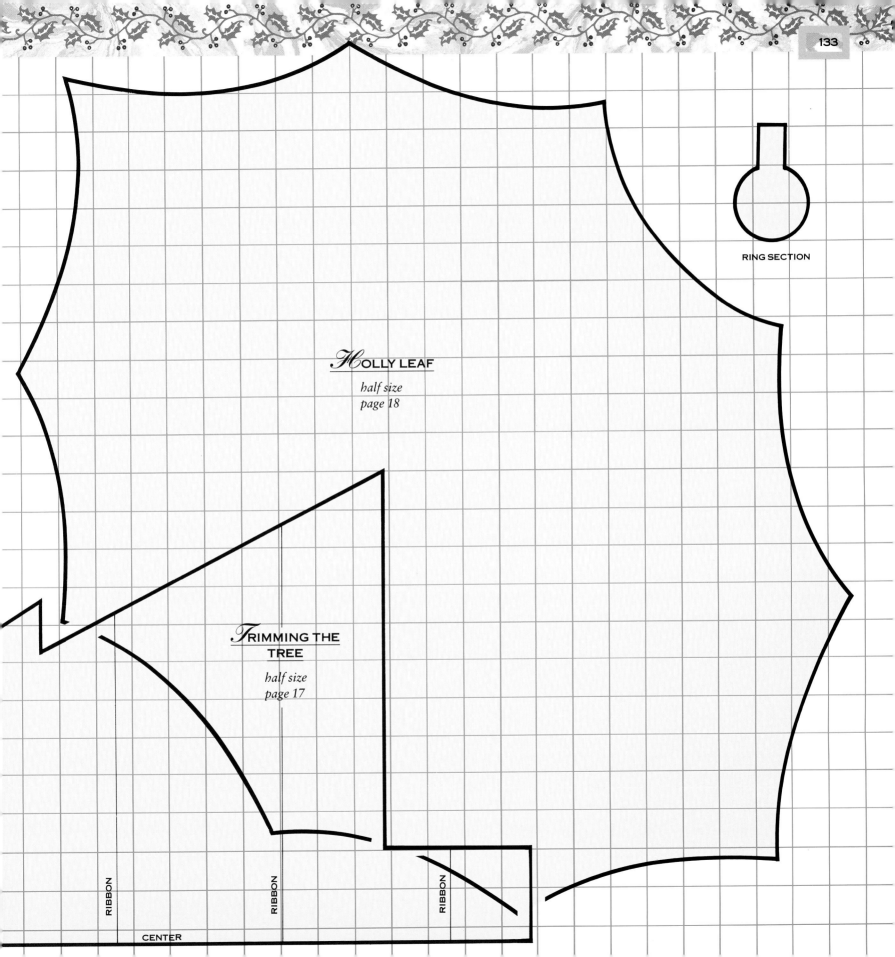

RING SECTION

*H*OLLY LEAF

half size
page 18

*T*RIMMING THE
TREE

half size
page 17

RIBBON

RIBBON

RIBBON

CENTER

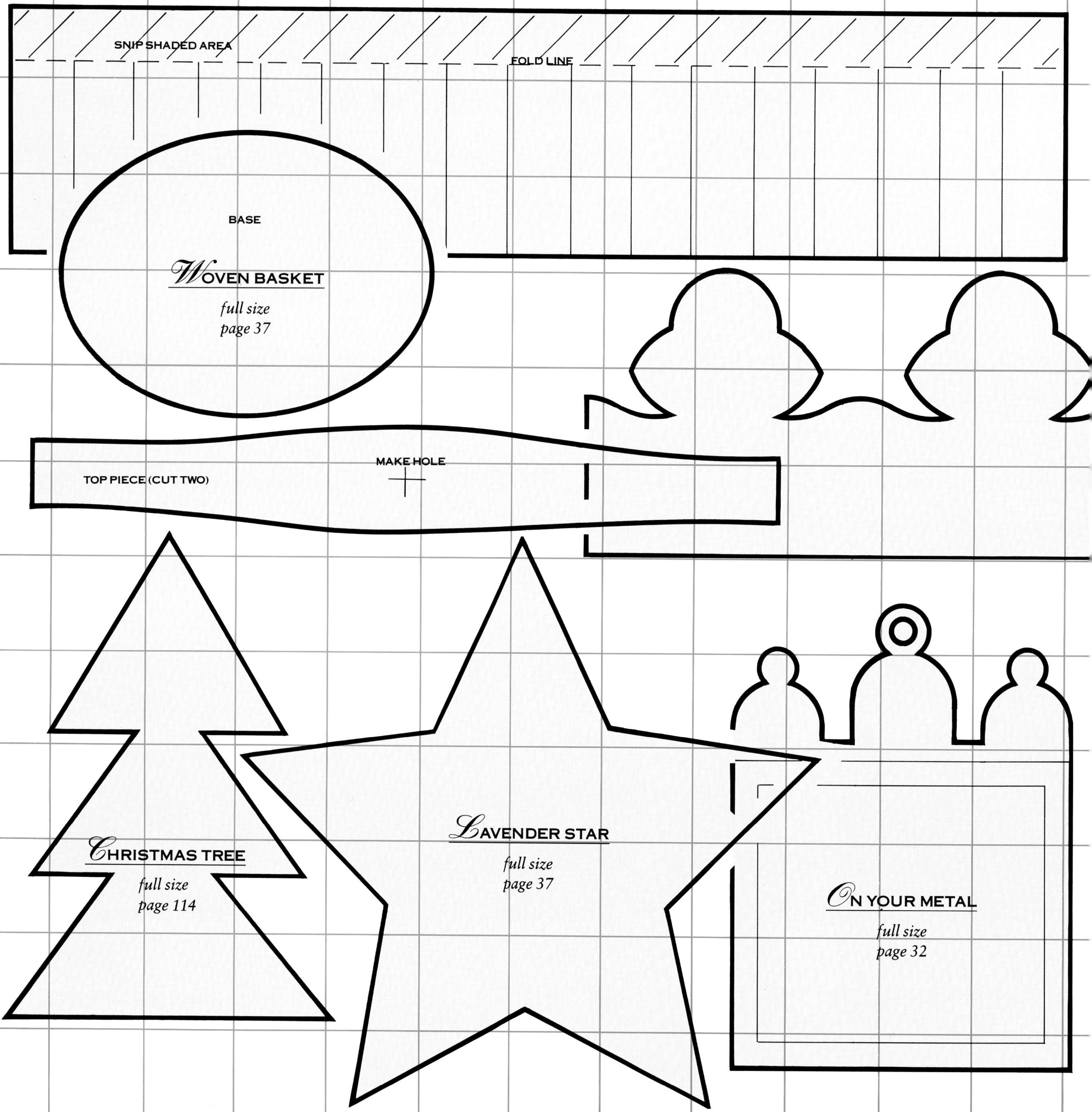

SNIP SHADED AREA

FOLD LINE

BASE

*W*OVEN BASKET

full size
page 37

MAKE HOLE

TOP PIECE (CUT TWO)

*C*HRISTMAS TREE

full size
page 114

*L*AVENDER STAR

full size
page 37

*O*N YOUR METAL

full size
page 32

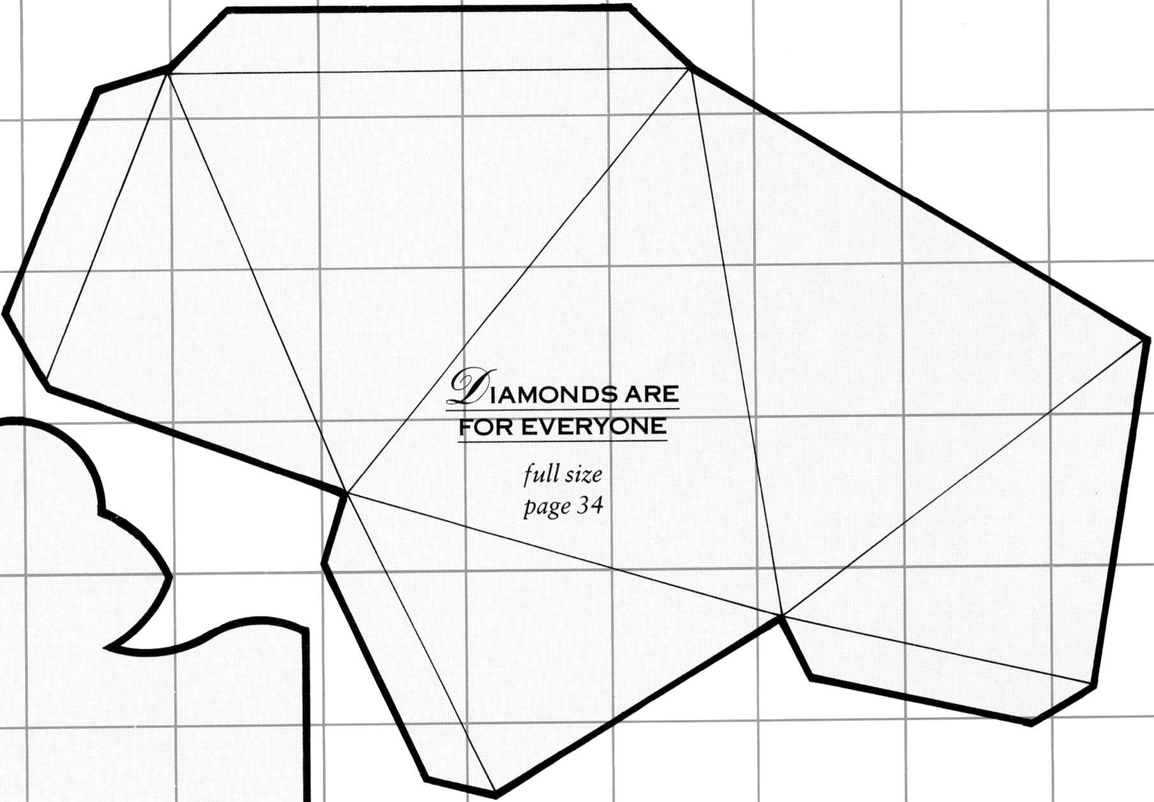

DIAMONDS ARE
FOR EVERYONE

*full size
page 34*

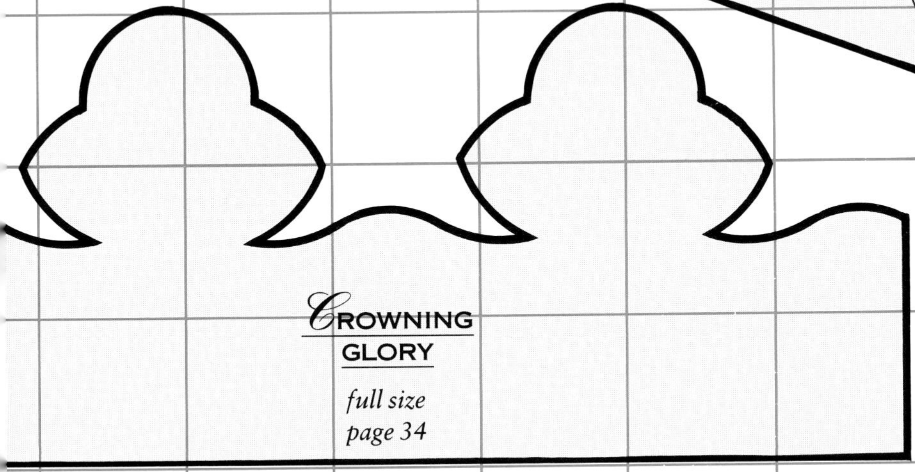

CROWNING
GLORY

*full size
page 34*

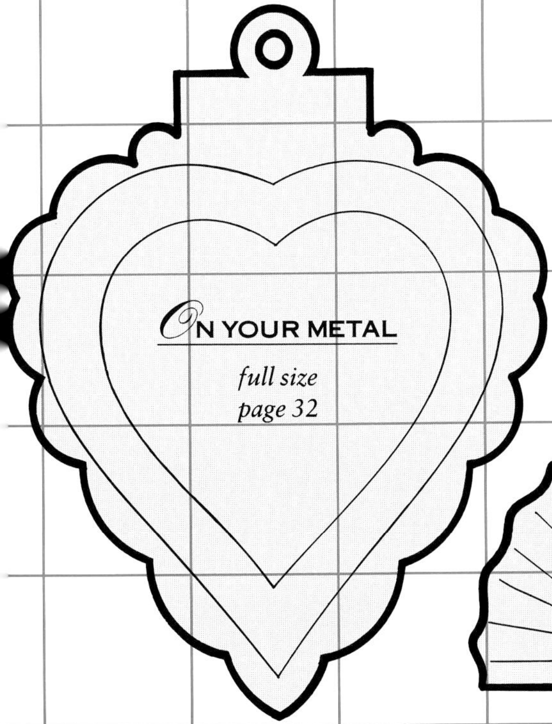

ON YOUR METAL

*full size
page 32*

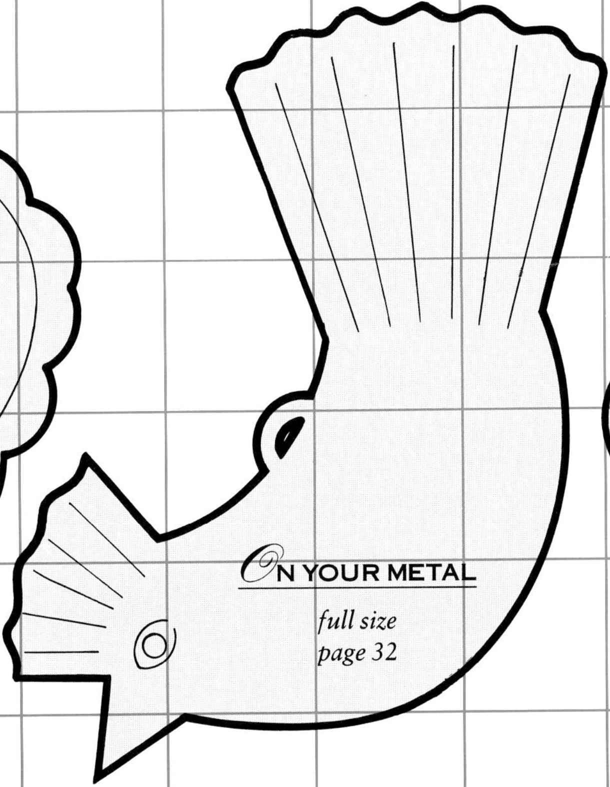

ON YOUR METAL

*full size
page 32*

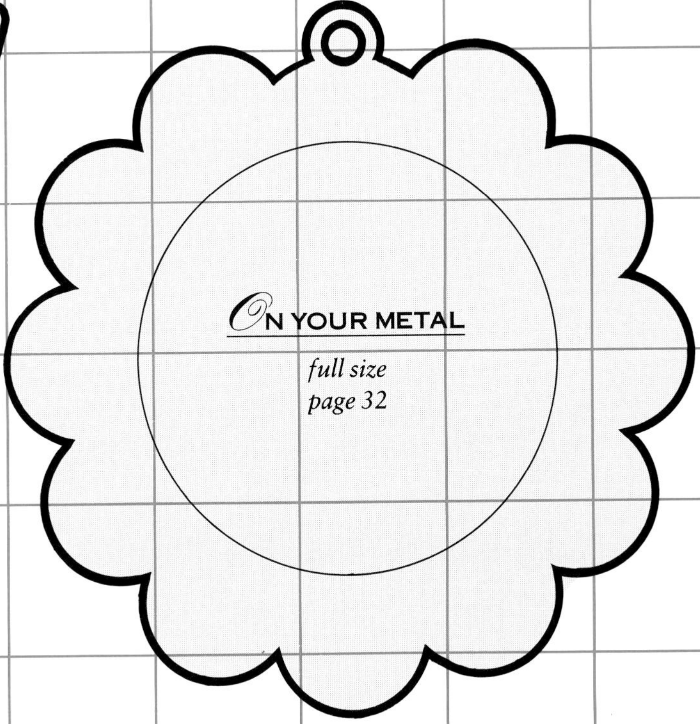

ON YOUR METAL

*full size
page 32*

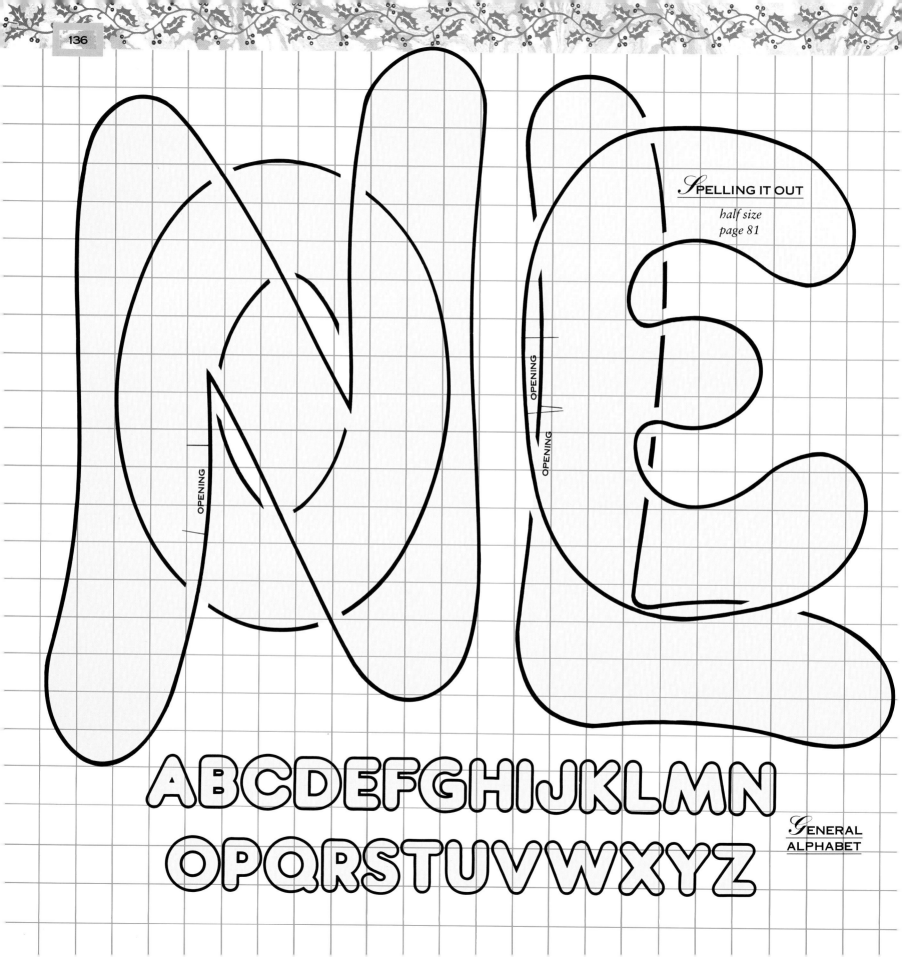

*S*PELLING IT OUT

half size
page 81

OPENING

OPENING

OPENING

ABCDEFGHIJKLMN
OPQRSTUVWXYZ

*G*ENERAL
ALPHABET

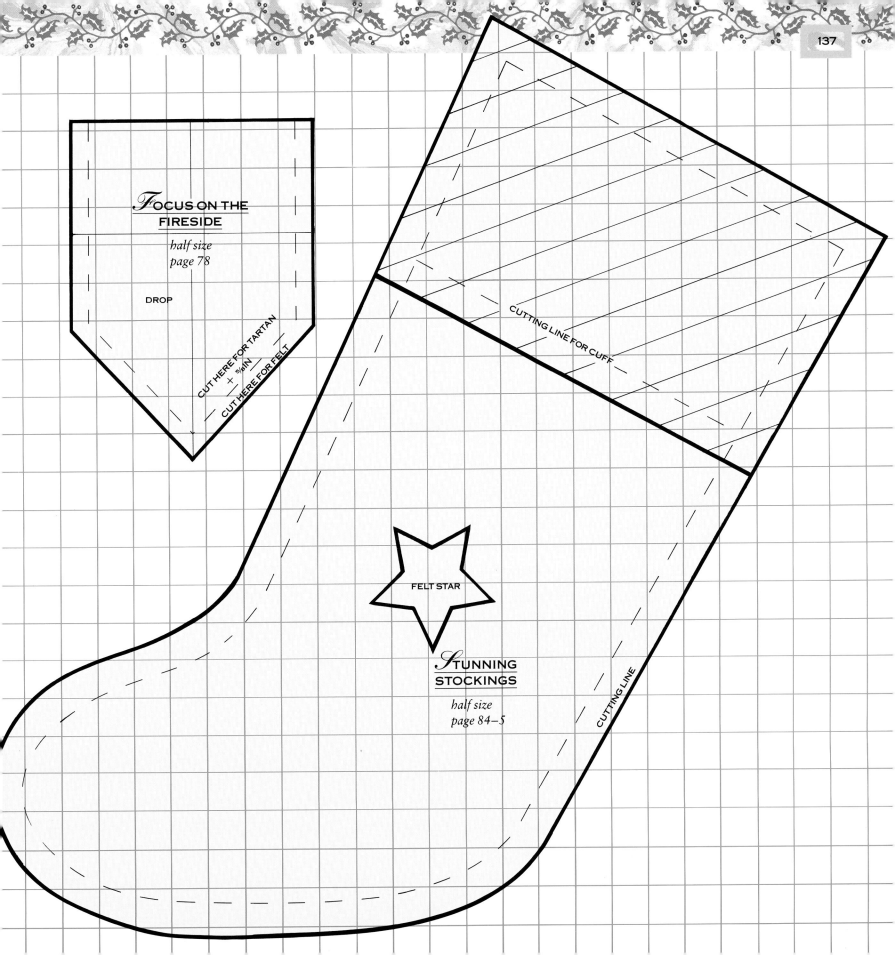

Focus ON THE FIRESIDE

half size
page 78

DROP

CUT HERE FOR TARTAN
+ ⅝IN
CUT HERE FOR FELT

CUTTING LINE FOR CUFF

FELT STAR

Stunning STOCKINGS

half size
page 84–5

CUTTING LINE

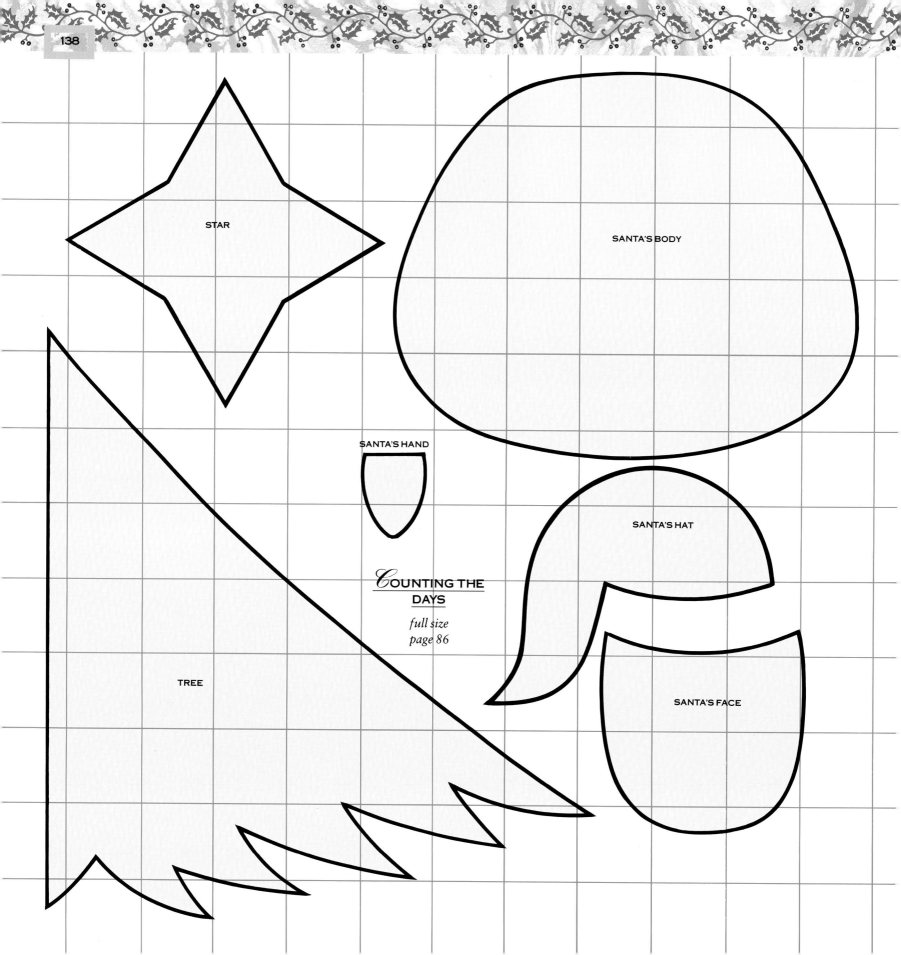

STAR

SANTA'S BODY

SANTA'S HAND

SANTA'S HAT

COUNTING THE
DAYS

*full size
page 86*

TREE

SANTA'S FACE

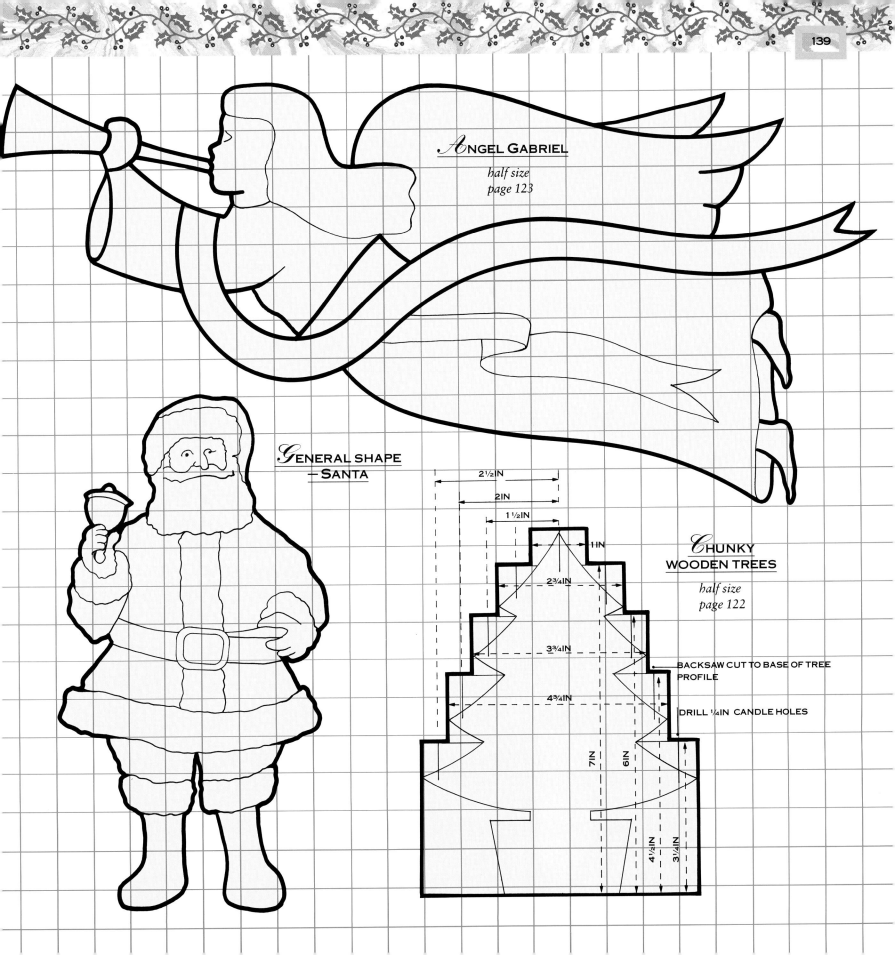

Angel Gabriel

half size
page 123

General Shape
— Santa

Chunky
Wooden Trees

half size
page 122

2½IN

2IN

1½IN

1IN

2¾IN

3¾IN

4¾IN

BACKSAW CUT TO BASE OF TREE
PROFILE

DRILL ¼IN CANDLE HOLES

7IN

6IN

4½IN

3¼IN

GLOSSARY

CLASSIC BOW

To make a classic bow, fold a length of ribbon into two loops. Now cross one loop over the other and make a knot by pushing it through the hole. Pull tight. Cut the two tails into an inverted V-shape.

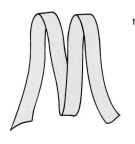

1

2

3

CLIPPING CURVES

To be able to press open a curved seam properly, you need to first clip the

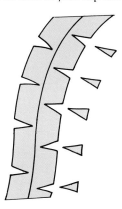

curve within the seam allowance at regular intervals. Clip to within about $1/16$in of the stitching, being careful not to clip through it. On outward curves, clip into the seam allowance and on inward curves cut out small notches.

COTTON BALLS

Molded balls known as "cotton balls" are very lightweight and are ideal for tree ornaments. They come in various sizes.

CUTTING ON THE BIAS

Fabric cut on the bias grain is cut on the diagonal between the lengthwise and crosswise threads. Fabric cut on the bias is stretchier than fabric cut on the straight grain.

DOUBLE BOW

To make a double bow, you'll need two loops and a straight length of ribbon, and another length of either the same or a contrasting ribbon. Tie the loops and matching length together

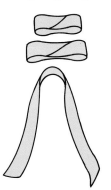

1

2

3

using the other length, and cut the two tails into an inverted V-shape.

GATHERING

Gathering is a way of adding fullness to fabric. Sew two parallel rows of stitching, one just inside the seamline and one just outside it. This can either be running stitch sewn by hand or a long straight stitch sewn by machine. When hand stitching, knot one end of each gathering thread and leave the other loose. When machine stitching, leave both ends of each thread loose. Now hold the gathering threads at one end (holding the bobbin threads if machine stitching has been used) and gently distribute the fullness evenly along the

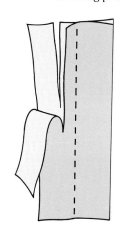

threads. Avoid jerking the threads or they could break.

GILDING, SIMULATED

Simulate gilding with bronzing powder (a finely ground alloy of brass, copper, or tin) for a smooth, glowing finish that is more subtle than metallic paint. First apply a transparent metallic-paint medium (alternatively, use clear glue, varnish, or gold-size). When it is sticky, dust the bronzing powder onto it; this technique is known as "pouncing." (As the powder is very fine, be sure to wear a mask while pouncing!)

GRADING SEAMS

Seam allowances that are turned in one direction rather than being pressed

open should be graded so that they will not be too bulky, especially if the fabric is heavy or there are more than two layers. Grading a seam simply involves cutting the layers of the seam allowance to different widths.

MITERING A SQUARE CORNER

To miter a square corner, first press the seam allowances to the inside. Now turn the corner to the inside diagonally

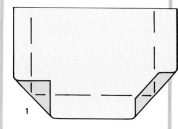

1

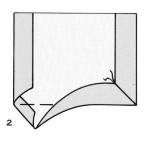

2

across the point where the two stitching lines meet. Press, then trim the seam allowance to $3/8$in. Slip-stitch.

MITERING THE CORNER OF A BINDING STRIP

Mitering is used to eliminate bulk at corners. To miter a binding strip before it is applied, pin it in place then mark the outer corner with a pin placed parallel to the edge. Remove the band. At the marked point, fold the band with right sides together, then turn the fold back as shown; press. Open out this diagonal fold and stitch along the crease. Trim to ⅛in. Press the seam open.

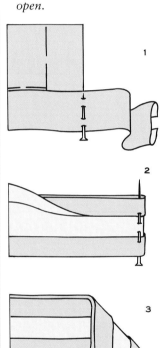

PAINTS

The majority of the paints used in this book are water-based, and are to some extent interchangeable.

WATERCOLORS
Transparent water-soluble paint, suitable for delicate effects. The cheaper ranges are fine for the projects here.

GOUACHE
An opaque version of watercolor, and about the same price. They are water-soluble, but can be varnished to make them more durable.

POSTER COLORS
Similar to gouache paints but runnier, and considerably less expensive. The colors are very bright and dry to a matte finish. An ideal "all-rounder" if you only want to buy one kind of paint.

POWDER PAINTS
The least expensive of all paints. They must be mixed with water before use, and the colors are slightly chalky. Suitable for large areas rather than fine work.

ACRYLIC PAINTS
These can be used undiluted or with water, but once dry form a tough plastic coating which cannot be removed. They are thus ideal for any items that will need washing or cleaning.

SPRAY PAINTS
These acrylic paints are fast-drying and give a sheen finish. They can be used on most surfaces and are especially useful where using a brush is difficult. Apply them in short, sharp bursts, building up the color gradually to avoid overspraying.

RUNNING STITCH

This stitch can be used for hand-gathering. Knot one end, then, working from right to left, pass the needle in and out of the fabric, taking several

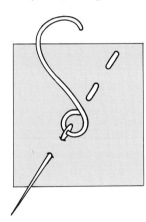

stitches before pushing the needle through. For gathering, the stitches should be ¹/₁₆–¹/₄in long. Leave the other end loose rather than fastening it off.

SLIP-STITCH

This stitch is reasonably invisible and can be used for joining two folded edges. It is useful if something has to be sewn from the right side. Knot the thread and bring the thread through one of the folds so the

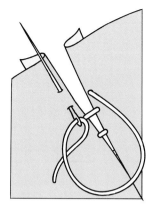

knot is hidden inside it. Working from right to left, take a small stitch along the fold, picking up only a thread or two, then take another in the fold opposite but about ¹/₁₆in further along. Continue in this manner.

STENCILING

Oiled manila cardboard or acetate is used for cutting out stencils. Oiled manila card is preferable as it is much easier to cut with a craft knife; acetate tends to split. Use carbon paper and a sharp pencil to transfer designs onto it.

TOP-STITCHING

This is normally straight machine stitching which is used decoratively. Work from the right side, and use a long stitch.

WIRED BOW

To make a traditional wired bow, make a loop by crossing one end of a length of ribbon over the front of the rest. Bring the remaining portion of the ribbon over that to form a second loop. Double that back on itself to form a third loop lying above the first one. Make a fourth loop in the same way, so that it lies above the second one. Pleat the center of the bow and tie with fine wire (or narrow ribbon). Cut the two ends into inverted V-shapes.

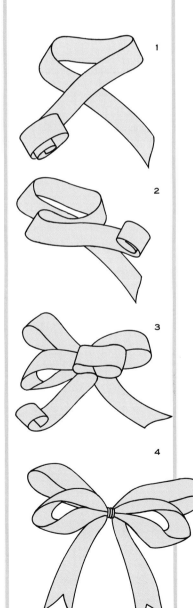

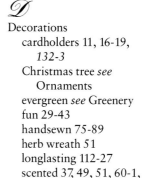

*A*CKNOWLEDGMENTS

The publishers would like to thank all the craftspeople who contributed to the book:

10 bl Jane Newdick, br Janet Slingsby; 11 l Hilary More, r Jane Newdick; 12–15 Emma Hardy; 16–19 Hilary More; 20 bl and br Jane Newdick, t Emma Hardy; 22–7 Jane Newdick; 30 Gloria Nicol; 31 tl Deborah Schneebeli-Morrell, br Emma Hardy; 32–3 Deborah Schneebeli-Morrell; 34–7 Gloria Nicol; 38–41 Emma Hardy; 42–3 Hilary More; 44–5 Jane Newdick; 48 Moira Clinch; 49 tl Gloria Nicol, bl Annemarie Rosier, tr Moira Clinch; 50–9 Gloria Nicol; 60–1 Annemarie Rosier (potpourri and fragrant paper flowers), Jane Newdick (pomanders and spice balls); 62–3 Jane Newdick; 64–5 Annemarie Rosier; 66–73 Jane Newdick; 76 Hilary More; 77 l Jane Newdick, r Hilary More; 78–81 Hilary More; 82–85 Gloria Nicol; 86–7 Hilary More; 88–9 Helen Milosavljevich; 90–1 Jane Newdick; 94 Hilary More; 95 bl Gloria Nicol, tr Emma Hardy; 96–7 Emma Hardy; 98–100 Helen Milosavljevich; 102–7 Gloria Nicol; 108–9 Hilary More; 110–11 Jane Newdick; 114 l Annemarie Rosier, r Hilary More; 115 Annemarie Rosier; 116 Mary Straka; 117 Annemarie Rosier; 118–9 Janet Slingsby; 120–1 Hilary More, Jane Newdick (shell candles); 122–3 John Burke, Simon Cavelle (paint finish for angel); 124–5 Annemarie Rosier; 126–7 Hilary More

The publishers would also like to thank the following companies and individuals:

11, 16–17, 18–19 Debbie Harter, **Robot Design Ltd**, Brighton ("Turtle Doves" and "Partridge in a Pear Tree" cards)

16–17, 18–19 **Plum Graphics Inc.**, New York (cat, tree and star cutout cards)

18–19 **Greetings Graphics**, Los Angeles (Christmas tree card)

2–3, 57, 78–9 wallpaper supplied by **Osborne & Little plc**, London

Fireplaces supplied by **Amazing Grates**, London N2

2–3, 57, 103 chinaware and glassware provided by and available from **House of Chinacraft**, 198 Regent St, London W1 and branches

42 **Hallmark Cards**, Henley-on-Thames, Oxon RG9 1LQ (shiny paper)

Ribbons for Hilary More's projects supplied by **Panda Ribbons**, Stoke-on-Trent ST8 7RM

115tl, 124–5 (step-by-steps) photography by Tim and Zoë Hill

Index by Alison Wormleighton